Wayfaring

Wayfaring

Essays
Pleasant
and
Unpleasant

Alan Jacobs

William B. Eerdmans Publishing Company

Grand Rapids, Michigan / Cambridge, U.K.

Published 2010 by
Wm. B. Eerdmans Publishing Co.
2140 Oak Industrial Drive N.E., Grand Rapids, Michigan 49505 /
P.O. Box 163, Cambridge CB3 9PU U.K.

Printed in the United States of America

15 14 13 12 11 10   7 6 5 4 3 2 1

Library of Congress Cataloging-in-Publication Data

Jacobs, Alan, 1958-
Wayfaring: essays pleasant and unpleasant / Alan Jacobs.
p.   cm.
ISBN 978-0-8028-6568-7 (pbk.: alk. paper)
1. Christianity and literature.   I. Title.

PN49.J3147   2010
809'.933823 — dc22

2010006419

www.eerdmans.com

For Ashley and Mary, with love

Contents

2. Signs and Wonders

Introduction

FROM THE first page of Charles Lamb's essay of 1823 on "Poor Relations":

> He is known by his knock. Your heart telleth you "That is Mr. — ."
> A rap, between familiarity and respect; that demands, and, at the
> same time, seems to despair of entertainment. He entereth smil-
> ing, and — embarrassed. He holdeth out his hand to you to shake,
> and draweth it back again. He casually looketh in about dinner
> time — when the table is full. He offereth to go away, seeing you
> have company — but is induced to stay. He filleth a chair, and your
> visitor's two children are accommodated at a side table.

This is Lamb's typical wry brightness of tone. As the essay moves
along, and as Lamb catalogues the varieties of poor relations, he finds
himself recalling a boy he had known as a student at Christ's Hospital
— the old and venerable school in London that Coleridge also attended
— and also at Oxford. This young man, whom Lamb does not name,
had to leave the university without a degree because of his poverty. His
options were few and unpleasant; he enlisted in the Army, and was
killed in his first military action. Having told this story, Lamb seems to
pause a moment and then says,

> I do not know how, upon a subject which I began with treating
> half seriously, I should have fallen upon a recital so eminently

painful; but this theme of poor relationship is replete with so much matter for tragic as well as comic associations, that it is difficult to keep the account distinct without blending.

Of all the many virtues of the essay as a form, it seems to be that the most wonderful of them is exhibited here. It is what I have elsewhere called a humble mutability of tone, a willingness to acknowledge and accept the vagaries of the mind, with its habit of following its own pathways in serene disregard of what we would have it do. Lamb may have meant to write a comical bagatelle; his mind, it turned out, contained a store of memories that would not confine themselves to the mood in which he began.

Now, Lamb certainly could have insisted on regaining control of his enterprise. He could have returned to what he had written and brought forth the Great Leveling Hand of Revision and made his essay more consistent in theme and tone. But he did not do this. He did not do this, I think, because whatever point he had in mind when he began, the point of the essay had, in the process of writing it, *become* this surprising and discomfiting recognition that "this theme of poor relationship is replete with so much matter for tragic as well as comic associations, that it is difficult to keep the account distinct without blending." It is just this "blended" character of our experience of others, in which the tragic and the comic can never be stopped from blundering haplessly into one another's territory, that the essay ends up portraying. Or rather, one might say that the essay does not portray the blending itself so much as one man's unexpected and unlooked-for *recognition* of the blending. What is represented here is the mind — following in its habitual way its branching pathways of memory and reflection — discovering something deeply true that the mind's owner would just as soon not know.

Here's another example, from the beginning of that greatest of English essays, Virginia Woolf's *A Room of One's Own*. Woolf has been asked to give a talk on "women and fiction," and as she strolls, deep in contemplation of this topic, across the grounds of an Oxbridge college, an idea comes to her. It is like catching a fish, she thinks.

But however small it was, it had, nevertheless, the mysterious property of its kind — put back into the mind, it became at once very exciting, and important; and as it darted and sank, and flashed hither and thither, set up such a wash and tumult of ideas that it was impossible to sit still. It was thus that I found myself walking with extreme rapidity across a grass plot. Instantly a man's figure rose to intercept me. Nor did I at first understand that the gesticulations of a curious-looking object, in a cut-away coat and evening shirt, were aimed at me. His face expressed horror and indignation. Instinct rather than reason came to my help, he was a Beadle; I was a woman. This was the turf; there was the path. Only the Fellows and Scholars are allowed here; the gravel is the place for me. Such thoughts were the work of a moment. As I regained the path the arms of the Beadle sank, his face assumed its usual repose, and though turf is better walking than gravel, no very great harm was done. The only charge I could bring against the Fellows and Scholars of whatever the college might happen to be was that in protection of their turf, which has been rolled for 300 years in succession, they had sent my little fish into hiding.

What idea it had been that had sent me so audaciously trespassing I could not now remember.

In another genre — in a treatise, let us say — an idea lost is no idea at all. An idea lost returns to the realm of non-being from which it had so briefly emerged. It is nothing, and how can one include nothing in one's treatise? But for Woolf the idea lost is, if not an idea anymore, an experience — and an experience deeply relevant to the theme of women and fiction, because within these pages this is the first in a series of *interruptions* — and, as Woolf says later in describing the conditions in which women who wish to write fiction must labor, "Interruptions there will always be."

Let me give you one more quotation, from D. T. Max, in a recent *New Yorker* biographical essay on David Foster Wallace:

His novels were overstuffed with facts, humor, digressions, silence, and sadness. He conjured the world in two-hundred-word sentences that mixed formal diction and street slang, technicalese and plain speech; his prose slid forward with a controlled lack of control that mimed thought itself. "What goes on inside is just too fast and huge and all interconnected for words to do more than barely sketch the outlines of at most one tiny little part of it at any given instant," he wrote in "Good Old Neon," a story from 2001. Riffs that did not fit into his narrative he sent to footnotes and endnotes, which he liked, he once said, because they were "almost like having a second voice in your head."

I have come to think that this is the most remarkable aspect of Wallace's fiction: his tendency not to dispense with the intellectual and experiential materials that went into the making of the story proper, but rather to incorporate those materials into the book, setting them at some distance from, and at angles to, the main narrative thrust. I find this fascinating, perhaps because I am drawn to anything essayistic.

In contrast to *Infinite Jest,* a book like Joyce's *Ulysses,* say, is not essayistic: there's a world of difference between the pathways of the mind that Wallace (and in their different ways Lamb and Woolf) trace and what Joyce called the "blooming, buzzing confusion" of sensory impressions. And yet "sensory impressions" are part of the story I'm telling too. The essay would be a limited form indeed if it could only tell us about the pathways our minds follow without reference to our bodies.

Consider Montaigne's reflections, in what I believe to be the finest essay ever written, "Of Repentance," on growing older:

> I hate that accidental repentance that old age brings. The man who said of old that he was obliged to the years for having rid him of sensuality had a different viewpoint from mine; I shall never be grateful to impotence for any good it may do me. . . . Miserable sort of remedy, to oue our health to disease! . . . Therefore I renounce these casual and painful reformations.
>
> God must touch our hearts. Our conscience must reform by itself through the strengthening of our reason, not through the weakening of our appetites. Sensual pleasure is neither pale nor colorless in itself for being seen through dim and blary eyes. WE should love temperance for itself and out of reverence toward God, who has commanded it, and also chastity; what catarrh lends

us, and what I owe to the favor of my colic, is neither chastity nor temperance. We cannot boast of despising and fighting sensual pleasure, if we do not see or know it, and its charms, its powers, and its most alluring beauty.

I love this because it is so honest, so unsentimental, and so gently comical. Montaigne knows — better than any writer I can think of except perhaps W. H. Auden — that having a body is really kind of funny, and a constant affront to our pretenses to dignity. St. Francis understood this too, which is why he referred to his body as Brother Ass.

(And note, by the way, how we literary critics and continental-philosophy types like to talk about "the body" — you know, The Body: the proper-nouned abstraction has much more *gravitas* than plain old bodies, the kinds that even literary critics and continental philosophers have. The educational guru Ken Robinson once commented that academics think of their bodies as vehicles for getting their heads to meetings. The more you think about The Body, the less you have to think about *your* body.)

So the paths of the mind, seen honestly, are often paths set by our bodies. This is a particularly interesting fact in light of the fact that so many essays — devoted as they are to following the paths of thought — are built on memories. The cognitive scientist Antonio Damasio has argued that our memories are accompanied by what he calls "somatic markers" — neural encodings of the various physical conditions (sensory, hormonal) that existed in our bodies at the moment that the remembered event happened. So to recall an event is to retrieve the whole somatic context of that event: remembering a moment of fear, we shiver; remembering excitement, we blush.

This is a reminder of how little we control our own experiences, try though we might. And how little we control the paths we follow, whether neurally or in the great metaphorical sense of life as a pilgrimage — of a person as a *viator,* a wayfarer. I love the essay primarily because it is the genre *par excellence* of wayfaring.

An old phrase holds that to be a Christian is to be *homo viator:* the human being as wayfarer, as pilgrim. Wayfarers know in a general sense where we are headed: to the City of God, what John Bunyan, that great chronicler of pilgrimage, called the Celestial City — but we aren't altogether certain of the way. We can get lost for a time, or lose our focus and nap for too long on a soft patch of grass at the side of the road, or dally a few days at Vanity Fair. We can even become discouraged — but we don't, ultimately and finally, give up. And we don't think we have arrived. To presume that we have made it to our destination and to despair of arriving are both, as Jürgen Moltmann has wisely said, ways of "canceling the wayfaring character of hope."

Hope comes from knowing that there is a way — and that we didn't make it. This is why the road's unexpected turnings need not alarm us; this is why it's possible even to enjoy the unpredictable, whether it comes from without or within. That is, there can be pleasure and instruction in the books we stumble across, in the serendipitous skipping from link to link across the Web — and even in our own mental vagaries, the stumbling and skipping through our neural webs.

Of course, what is instructive is not always pleasurable, and what is pleasurable is not always instructive. That's life. So, just as George Bernard Shaw wrote what he called *Plays Pleasant and Unpleasant,* these are Essays Pleasant and Unpleasant. Some are celebratory, some are critical; most partake of both attitudes. You never know what kinds of things will turn up along the way.

"Sentences" and "A Commonplace Book" appeared on the website of *Books & Culture* magazine, as part of a monthly online column called Rumors of Glory. "Bran Flakes and Harmless Drudges," "The Poet's Prose," "Opportunity Costs," "The Youngest Brother's Tale," "The Life of Trees," "Gardening and Governing," and "Choose Life" all appeared in the print edition of *Books & Culture.*

"Robert Alter's Fidelity," "A Religion for Atheists," "On the Recent Publication of Kahlil Gibran's Collected Works," "Reading the Signs," "The Secret Garden," "Blessed Are the Green of Heart," and "Do-It-Yourself Tradition" all appeared in *First Things.*

I am deeply grateful to John Wilson of *Books & Culture* and Jody Bottum of *First Things* for providing homes for these pieces. "The End of Friendship" — an earlier version of which was delivered as a lecture at Baylor University — and "The Brightest Heaven of Invention" appear in print for the first time here.

Part 1

WORLDS OF READING

Sentences

IN HER wonderful book *The Writing Life,* Annie Dillard tells this anecdote:

> A well-known writer got collared by a university student who asked, 'Do you think I could be a writer?'
>
> "Well," the writer said, "I don't know . . . Do you like sentences?"

Since I first read this story many years ago, I have thought that the unnamed author — was it Dillard herself? — gave one of the best possible answers to that eternal question. For writing, the writing of prose anyway, is largely a matter of making sentences: hammering one together, connecting it to another, eventually framing a whole edifice. But one sentence at a time is the only way you can do it.

I may not be much of a writer, but I do like sentences; indeed I love them, and think about them a lot — shockingly often, really. I am one of the few remaining Americans blessed with the opportunity to walk to and from work each day, and as I walk I am likely to be rolling sentences around in my head. I have even stopped listening to *This American Life* on my iPod, the better to facilitate concentration. Sometimes, when I want extra time to consider my options — the walk is only about fifteen minutes — I take a detour to Starbucks. I enjoy the coffee, but I'm really just prolonging my commute for the sake of the sentences.

I am not sure that this obsession is wholly healthy. Not long ago I was writing an essay in which I planned to say a few words about a critic named Ilan Stavans, and I thought it appropriate to note that Stavans has a curious cultural situation: he was born Ilan Stavchansky, not in Russia or New York or anywhere else you might expect someone with such a name to grow up, but in Mexico City. As a boy he attended a Yiddish school there, and now — he teaches at Amherst College — he seems to live at the intersections of the Yiddish, Spanish, and English languages. (You can learn more about Stavans's internal multicultural-ism in his fine book, *On Borrowed Words: A Memoir of Language*.) All these reflections were appropriate, I thought, because the essay was about dictionaries, about language. But I found myself also wanting, perhaps without so much justification, to note that Stavans looks, in one photo anyway, rather like the actor Nick Nolte.

Now, at the time that I made the Nolte connection, I didn't know that Stavans was born Stavchansky; I wasn't sure what to make of the name Stavans. I just knew that he grew up in Mexico City and was Jewish. So I started trying to make a sentence based on my imperfect knowledge. Eventually I came up with something like this: "You wouldn't think Stavans was Jewish or Mexican, any more than you would think Nick Nolte (whom, to judge by the author photo on *Dictionary Days,* Stavans resembles) was Jewish or Mexican." But, I started asking myself, is that awkward? Does the parenthesis carry the point strongly enough? Perhaps I should use dashes instead. Now, "whom" — that's accurate, but it will *sound* wrong to some readers — should I rephrase? Maybe I should break the whole thing into two sentences, though getting it all into one sentence is the challenge, and therefore part of the fun . . .

Lost in verbal carpentry, I did not for some time reflect that what the sentence *said* was probably not something I should commit to print. Of course, I was trying to make a little joke, but the reward of getting a smile from one or two readers was not worth the risk of sounding like a bigot: "Gee, he doesn't *look* Mexican! He doesn't *look* like a Jew!" Be-sides — the non-sentence-making portions of my brain creaked into ac-tion — Nick Nolte, though he looks pretty Northern European, did after all play an Italian in *Lorenzo's Oil* . . . and come to think of it, one of the reasons Stavans looks like Nolte is that his eyeglasses resemble the ones that Nolte wore in that movie. But wait: *was* it in that movie that Nolte wore the glasses? Maybe it was some other film.

At this point it was obvious that the amount of research into film history and Nick Nolte's genealogy that I would have to do in order to justify the sentence made the sentence worse than useless to me, even if it *didn't* make me sound like a bigot. But the problem of how to make that point, how to construct that sentence, continued to occupy my walks to and from work long after I had decided that I wasn't even going to mention Stavans in my essay. It had detached itself from the world of purpose and meaning, and become a purely formal exercise in rhythm, balance, and the possibility of elegance. It was driving me nuts, but I couldn't let it go, and after a time I began to reflect that I was acting like a mathematician trying to solve something like Fermat's Last Theorem — except that for solving Fermat's Last Theorem Andrew Wiles won a lucrative prize and international renown, whereas for solving the Ilan Stavans/Nick Nolte Problem I would win nothing but a reputation for ethnic insensitivity.

Alas, it's not just my own sentences that occupy me thus: I can get just as occupied by the equally pointless challenge of rewriting the sentences of others. For instance, in his book *How Soccer Explains the World* Franklin Foer gives us this: "Barcelona fans threw projectiles on the field, including sandwiches, fruit, golf balls, mobile phones, whiskey bottles, bike chains, and a severed bloody boar's head." Now, when I read that sentence this was my first and virtually my only thought: Should it really be "severed bloody boar's head"? That doesn't sound right. How about "bloody severed boar's head"? — no, that's not any better, probably because of the unnecessary information: if you have a bloody boar's head to throw, doesn't it go without saying that it has been severed? I mean, otherwise you'd just have a whole boar, wouldn't you? Clearly, the sentence would have been stronger had it ended, ". . . whiskey bottles, bike chains, and a bloody boar's head." Yes! Much better!

This is perhaps not the path of sanity, or virtue either for that matter. John Updike was widely reviled, and rightly so I think, for using the collapse of the World Trade Center towers as an opportunity for making beautiful sentences: "Smoke speckled with bits of paper curled into the cloudless sky, and strange inky rivulets ran down the giant structure's vertically corrugated surface," he wrote in *The New Yorker;* one of the towers "fell straight down like an elevator, with a tinkling shiver and a groan of concussion distinct across the mile of air." Leon Wieseltier in *The New Republic* offered the most incisive critique of Updike's approach: "Such writing defeats its representational purpose, because it steals attention away from reality and toward language. It is provoked by nothing so much as its own delicacy. Its precision is a trick: it appears to bring the reader near, but it keeps the reader far. It is in fact a kind of armor: an armor of adjectives and adverbs. The loveliness is invincible." The great Chilean poet Pablo Neruda made the same point in one of his poems: "and the blood of children ran through the street / without fuss, like children's blood." Neruda, among the most metaphorically extravagant of poets, knew that in this case metaphor or simile would be obscene.

Similarly, Charles Williams once wrote, "When the means are autonomous, they are deadly." When the "means" of art, its various instruments, become detached from the human world of moral action and spiritual meaning, the damage they can do is beyond estimation. And yet the world is also full of people who, in their eagerness to tell the truth they see, ignore those instruments or employ them carelessly. It's vital to attend to the world as it is, refusing to don the armor of aestheticism; it's vital to use the "means" with the utmost skill and care, to be as vivid and elegant as possible. This is why writing is hard.

A Commonplace Book

A WHILE BACK, I started keeping a commonplace book. *Commonplace book* is an odd phrase, perhaps, because what you are supposed to record in such a book is, from one point of view, anything but commonplace. It's likely that, as long as people have been able to write, some have recorded memorable ideas, wise sayings, or beautiful lines of poetry — words of rare value, distinctive enough that we dare not trust them only to our memories.

It was in the sixteenth century, especially in England, that the practice of such recording became widespread and recommended by the learned to all thoughtful and literate persons. This happened for two reasons. First, in that time paper became more widely available and considerably cheaper than it had been — developments prompted by the invention of the printing press but beneficial to the private scribbler as well. And the printing press had another consequence: By making it so much faster and easier to disseminate texts of every kind — from Bibles (and commentaries thereon) to ghost stories, breathless accounts of notorious murders, and scurrilous poems on leading politicians — the world of print created a panic, the kind of panic distinctive to people who feel swamped by information.

Ann Blair is a historian at Harvard who has been exploring early-modern information overload, and her work — so far a handful of articles, though a book is on the way — wonderfully reveals the sheer anxiety of those readers. By the latter part of the seventeenth century, some people had come to believe that the constant onrushing freight of words was threatening to undermine European culture altogether: One Adrien Baillet wrote, "We have reason to fear that the multitude of books which grows every day in a prodigious fashion will make the following centuries fall into a state as barbarous as that of the centuries that followed the fall of the Roman Empire."

The commonplace book arose as a means of mastering or at least fighting off this "multitude of books." For much of the history of reading and writing, books have been rare and expensive things, enormously time-consuming to produce. Their owners therefore took good care of them, pored over them repeatedly until the words had been all but memorized, and passed them on to their children. Individual books are frequently mentioned in early wills; and, when the great tinker-turned-writer John Bunyan married, the dowry he received from his new father-in-law consisted of two popular devotional books. But in the sixteenth century, the relatively wealthy and those who lived in large cities found themselves with access to more books than they could read, or at any rate read with care. Thus the need to select the best and wisest passages from those books — passages that were commonplace in an etymological sense, from *locus communis,* the "communal place," the thing of general use and value — in short, the kind of writing that you expect will repay repeated consideration. A book full of such passages would be a treasure-house, something even worth passing on to your children.

It was probably inevitable that commonplace books would eventually blend with another early-modern invention, the journal. By 1720, when Jonathan Swift writes "A Letter of Advice to a Young Poet" and recommends the keeping of a commonplace book, he seems to have something very like a journal in mind: "A book of this sort, is in the nature of a supplemental memory, or a record of what occurs remarkable in every day's reading or conversation. There you enter not only your own original thoughts (which, a hundred to one, are few and insignificant) but such of other men as you think fit to make your own, by entering them there." It's interesting that Swift thinks that by writing down the thoughts and ideas of others you are "making them your own"; elsewhere in the letter he refers to such a book as a bank from which you can make withdrawals of wit and wisdom. As T. S. Eliot would later say, "Immature poets imitate; mature poets steal." Swift recommends theft.

My own commonplace book is of the earlier variety, in that it contains few words of my own: It is made up almost wholly of other people's writings — but also their images, still and moving, and sounds. For my book exists online: It is a Web phenomenon only, employing no paper. Ah, you say, you're referring to your blog! To which I reply, well, yes and no.

It is curious that the history of the weblog, insofar as it can be fully understood, mirrors that of the commonplace book. The term *weblog* seems to have been coined by a very strange man named Jorn Barger, and for him it is simply a log of interesting stories he discovers on the Web. It consists of links with brief descriptions, nothing more. But of course what most of us now think of when we use the word *blog* is a kind of online journal or diary; and that is indeed the path the weblog or blog has, generally speaking, followed. What was once a log of things other people said on the Web is now a log of my own life, which I make available to readers, and which may (but need not) contain links and references. So when we speak of blogs we don't mean what Jorn Barger does; we mean — well, something like what Jonathan Swift recommended to his young poet friend: "a record of what occurs remarkable in every day's reading [or viewing or iPod-listening] or conversation."

My commonplace book certainly isn't a blog in the sense of a diary or journal, since it doesn't feature my writing; it's closer to what Jorn Barger does but not identical to that either. The three or four words that Barger appends to his links tell us little about what, exactly, interested him in the linked article, what he thinks especially important or worthwhile. By contrast, I present excerpts from what I've been reading that I think capture the spirit of it; or, if it's a poem (I post a lot of poems), I give the whole thing. This is not primarily an act of courtesy to my readers, of whom I can't possibly have many, but rather an act of intellectual discipline on my part, whereby I hope to capture for my later reading self the significance of what I've posted.

(I should pause here to dispel any solemnity: I post and link to plenty of comical things as well. And, while I wouldn't post photos of me or my family, I do occasionally share images of my Shetland sheepdog, Malcolm. He's *really* cute.)

One could think in many different ways about how my commonplace book resembles or differs from those that emerged in the sixteenth century. Were I keeping my book on paper, with a pen, I would be making wise words "my own" by writing them out in my own script, my own "hand": This physical act of mimicry was something the early-modern world took quite seriously, though we do not. But should we? Select-cut-paste is a very different act from copying laboriously by hand, but how might that difference manifest itself in my mind?

Likewise, how, and how much, does it matter that my commonplace book is fully public, accessible by any stranger? And that it is not something that I can pass on to my son, at least not in a way recognizable to earlier book owners? There's no way for readers to comment on my book, which makes the environment a little less like a Hyde Park Corner harangue or an Iowa caucus; it brings me a little closer to those old anthologists, makes it more fully *mine*. (On the other hand, just this morning a reader took the trouble to find my email address and send me a message saying, "I love Malcolm!" And I didn't mind that at all.)

Some of these questions will not have clear answers anytime soon. The blog, in any and all of its variants, is quite a recent phenomenon, and in the long run we may well develop distinct terms for each of those variants, rather than lumping them all in a single catchall category. Bernard Williams, that fine philosopher, used to say that "we suffer from a poverty of concepts," and I think that that's certainly true in our discussions of life online: "Is the Internet good or bad for us?" is a meaningless question because there is no one thing called "the Internet." As our concepts for describing these cyberspatial interactions multiply and become more precise, we will be better equipped to understand how closely these forms of writing and reading resemble earlier ones.

In the meantime, I think I can hazard this claim: *Keeping* a commonplace book is easy, but *using* one? Not so much. I started my first one when I was a teenager, and day after day I wedged open books under a foot of my ancient Smith-Corona manual typewriter and banged out the day's words of wisdom. I had somewhat different ideas then of what counted as wisdom. The mainstays of that era — Arthur C. Clarke and Carl Sagan were perhaps the dominant figures — haven't made any appearances in my online world. But even then I suspected something that I now know to be true: The task of adding new lines and sentences and paragraphs to one's collection can become an ever tempting substitute for reading, marking, learning, and inwardly digesting what's already there. And wisdom that is not frequently revisited is wisdom wasted.

Robert Alter's Fidelity

As THE Italians say, *traduttori, tradittori:* translators are traitors. But the translator who shrugs and — cheerfully or resignedly — agrees that "every translation is an interpretation, after all" has too readily embraced the way of the *tradittore.* The translator who strives for strict fidelity, even knowing its elusiveness, will be less treacherous. In translation, fidelity is the ultimate imperative and trumps every other virtue: even clarity or readability.

Translators of the Bible seem often to forget this, if indeed they believe it at all. In the introduction to his extraordinary recent translation, *The Five Books of Moses,* Robert Alter points out that modern translations operate under the (perhaps unconscious) "feeling that the Bible, because of its canonical status, has to be made accessible — indeed, transparent — to all." Alter is certainly right that modern translators have this feeling, and obey it, but the Bible's "canonical status" is less to blame than a particular conception of how the Bible *functions* in the lives of believers.

Almost all modern translations into English — even versions like the recent "Tanakh Translation" of the Jewish Publication Society — owe something to the zeal of such early English Christian translators as John Wycliffe and William Tyndale and their belief that the Bible must be made clear to the common reader. Near the end of the fourteenth century Wycliffe wrote, "No man is so rude a scholar but that he may learn the gospel according to its simplicity." A century and a half later, Tyn-

12

dale would utter — or so reports John Foxe, in his *Acts and Monuments* (1583) — the same thought in more vivid language. Responding to a "divine, reputed for a learned man," who had criticized Tyndale's views on Scripture, the great translator declared, "If God spare my life, ere many years I will cause a boy that driveth the plough shall know more of the Scriptures than thou dost."

It is often said that Wycliffe and Tyndale believed in a characteristic Protestant idea called "the perspicuity of Scripture" — an effective denial that the Scriptures are secret or occult, accessible only to those with special training or institutional authority. Rather, in the words of the Westminster Confession of Faith, "those things which are necessary to be known, believed, and observed for salvation are so clearly propounded, and opened in some place of Scripture or other, that not only the learned, but the unlearned, in a due use of the ordinary means, may attain unto a sufficient understanding of them." Or, as Martin Luther tersely put it — evoking the scene on the road to Emmaus when the risen Christ "opened the Scriptures" to a pair of bewildered disciples — "Christ has opened our understanding to grasp the Scriptures."

Now, these authors were quick to admit that many particular *passages* in Scripture are, as Luther has it, "obscure and abstruse." "All things in Scripture are not alike plain in themselves," says Westminster, "nor alike clear unto all." Nevertheless, men like Wycliffe and Tyndale have often been *thought* to say something more radical — that, thanks to the work of the Holy Spirit, the *whole* of Scripture is transparent to the humble but earnest interpreter. Whether they believed this or not, many of their followers do; and later translators of Scripture have operated under the (again, often unconscious) assumption that the ideal experience of reading Scripture is one in which clarity manifests itself fully and immediately.

Undergirding this assumption is, I think, a memory of Christ's disturbing statement: "I thank you, Father, Lord of heaven and earth, that you have hidden these things from the wise and understanding and revealed them to little children." Does this suggest that any translation that presents more difficulties to the "little children" than to the "wise and understanding" is somehow un-Christian? The idea may seem absurd, but it would be unwise to underrate the pressure of such thoughts in an assertively egalitarian, democratizing, and anti-elitist culture like our own today. Only in such a culture would something like "dynamic equivalence" models of translation be developed, because dynamic equivalence — which encourages translators to ask how *we* in our time and place might say whatever the Bible is taken to say — allows one to deal with difficult passages in the original text not by translating them but by interpreting their obscurities out of existence. Such passages must be cleared away, whenever possible, in order to make the crooked places straight and the rough places plain. The simple and problem-free translation then offers itself as evidence of the simplicity and problem-freeness of the biblical text itself. The translators thus stand to their readers *in loco parentis:* The "little children" never have to know what struggles their scholarly fathers undertook in order to protect them from the agonies of interpretive confusion.

It is noteworthy that Tyndale never thought to adopt such a strategy, despite his concern that the boy at the plow know the Bible. He understood perfectly well that many of the English words a faithful translation required him to employ would be unknown to many of his readers; however, his response to this problem was not to use only common words but to append to his translation a glossary of difficult terms. (At a time when real dictionaries were unheard of, this was a brilliant and innovative solution. Alas, Tyndale did not live to implement it.) Otherwise, readers would be in the lamentable situation of being unable to distinguish Tyndale's words from those of the text; and if he intruded his own words — even if those words were meant only to clarify or explain the Bible's — he would, by his own lights, have become a traitor rather than a translator.

Likewise, Wycliffe, for all his faith in the power of boys who drive plows to know their Bibles, makes it clear that Scripture exhibits its clarity only to those who undergo the lengthy *intellectual* discipline of submitting to its authority: "The faithful whom he calls in meekness and humility of heart, whether they be clergy or laity, male or female, bending the neck of their inner man to the logic and style of Scripture will find in it the power to labour and the wisdom hidden from the proud." God indeed reveals to the "little children" what is hidden from the "wise and understanding," but transforming oneself into a little child is the arduous work of a lifetime. Christ's yoke is easy and his burden light, but we don't like bending our necks to receive it — and no translation, however it accommodates itself to our language and understanding, can change *that*.

In criticizing the various "dynamic equivalence" models of translation, I lament what Robert Alter calls "the heresy of explanation" — "the use of translation as a vehicle for *explaining* the Bible rather than representing it in another language, [which] in the most egregious instances . . . amounts to explaining away the Bible." But for Alter there is no simple, straightforward alternative model of translation that by the application of some supposedly "literal" equation can magically achieve fidelity. The situation is too complicated for that, especially when languages as different as Hebrew and English are involved.

The complexity is fully recognized and acknowledged by Alter, who in a long and distinguished career has written with authority about the history of the novel and about biblical literature. He is professor of Hebrew and Comparative Literature at Berkeley, and his climb up the sheer face of the pentateuchal mount resembles some of the great monuments of humanistic scholarship more than the work of the rabbis: His interest in Scripture is evidently literary and cultural. (Vladimir Nabokov's work on Pushkin's *Eugene Onegin* is probably the single closest analogue to what Alter achieves in *The Five Books of Moses*.) In the 1980s he wrote *The Art of Biblical Narrative* and *The Art of Biblical Poetry*, and with Frank Kermode edited *The Literary Guide to the Bible*. More recently he has turned his hand to translation, first of Genesis, then of the vast biblical tale (largely consisting of the two books of Samuel) that he calls *The David Story*, and now the whole of the Pentateuch. To his scholarly accomplishments he adds an elegant English style, and he seems as prepared as a scholar can be to address the philological, historical, and literary problems that arise when one contemplates representing an ancient Hebrew text in modern English.

What to do, for instance, with *waw*? No problem is more constant for the translator from the Hebrew. *Waw* is a particle, attached to the beginning of many clauses, that, if translated as a word, is usually translated as "and." The preface to the Tanakh translation, however, points out that in biblical Hebrew *waw* has "the force not only of 'and' but also of 'however,' 'but,' 'yet,' 'when,' and any number of other such words and particles, or none at all that can be translated into English."

Therefore, these translators say, "Always to render it as 'and' is to misrepresent the Hebrew rather than be faithful to it." In a sense this is surely true; on the other hand, to use many different words to translate a single particle whose variations in meaning must, in Hebrew, be determined by the context is also a misrepresentation, just of a different kind.

As a case study in such difficulties, Alter cites Genesis 24, which begins with Abraham commissioning a servant to find a wife for Isaac. Alter focuses on verses 16 to 20, in which the servant encounters the extraordinary hospitality of a beautiful young woman named Rebekah, and points out that this passage contains fifteen instances of *waw*. He points out that the Revised English Version uses only five "ands" in the passage (as does the Tanakh translation). Alter, by contrast, gives us "and" all fifteen times:

> And she came down to the spring and filled her jug and came back up. And the servant ran toward her and said, "Pray, let me sip a bit of water from your jug." And she said, "Drink, my lord," and she hurried and tipped down her jug on one hand and let him drink, and she let him drink his fill and said, "For your camels, too, I shall draw water until they drink their fill." And she hurried and emptied her jug into the trough, and she ran again to the well to draw water and drew water for all his camels.

Why does Alter do this? It is not because he is unaware of the many subtle variations of *waw*. Nor is it because he follows an iron law that a Hebrew word (or particle) must always be translated with the same English word; he does not in fact follow such a law. Rather, he wishes, first, to represent the repetitions that would have been very noticeable to anyone listening to this text being read aloud — which is how almost everyone who knew the story in ancient Israel would have encountered it, since literacy was uncommon and confined largely to the priestly orders. (Thus when, in the reign of King Josiah, the priest Hilkiah discovers the long-lost book of the Law, it is read aloud first to the king and then to the whole people.) Moreover, the repetition gives a certain urgency to the story: In precisely the same way, people telling a breathless tale in English even today will insert after every sentence an identical "and then . . . and then . . . and then."

But why does this passage call for such breathlessness? What's so remarkable about Rebekah's offering water to the servant and his camels? Alter points out that the text's early listeners would have known that "a camel after a long desert journey can drink as much as twenty-five gallons of water, and there are ten camels here whom Rebekah offers to water 'until they drink their fill.'" In an environment in which water was rare and highly prized, Rebekah's action marks her as a heroine of hospitality: Her generosity is as remarkable as her beauty.

But of course no translation, however faithful, can convey such information, can it? Ah, that's what *commentary* is for. In his remarkable book *Religious Reading,* Paul Griffiths describes the curious genre of writing we call "commentary." The genre originates in response to sacred writing, but eventually finds its way to other sorts of texts: legal, political, literary, and so on. Alter's reflections on the Pentateuch are evidently not the product of "religious reading": It is the *artistry* of the Scriptures that he is at greatest pains to stress, and both his translation and his commentary are at their best when they illuminate that artistry.

But, says Griffiths, to be a true commentary, a written work must exhibit three features: First, "some other work [must] be overtly present in it"; second, indications of the presence of that other work "should dominate" the commentary, "either quantitatively or qualitatively"; and third, the structure of the commentary, "the order in which material occurs in it, should be given to it by" that other work. Griffiths also makes the helpful suggestion that you can tell that a work is truly a commentary by excising all "direct quotation, paraphrase, and summary" of that other work from it: If the result is something senseless, you're dealing with a commentary. This point enables us to see why many works of biblical and literary criticism are not commentaries: They possess their own structures, their own arguments, and would not be rendered incomprehensible even by the excision of most of their references to the books they are supposedly about.

There is nothing wrong with such non-commentarial criticism, but it usually does not, and certainly need not, treat the "other work" with reverence: It does not consider the other work as a *master* work, while commentary does — even when it wants to overthrow the work that is currently, however lamentably, its master. (The passive-aggressive duplicity of much biblical commentary was seen with shocking clarity by Kierkegaard: "Christian scholarship is the Church's prodigious invention to defend itself against the Bible, to ensure that we can continue to be good Christians without the Bible coming too close. . . . We would be sunk if it were not for Christian scholarship! Praise be to everyone who works to consolidate the reputation of Christian scholarship, which helps to restrain the New Testament, this confounded book which would, one, two, three, run us all down if it got loose.")

It is a rare thing to find scholars willing not only to treat another text as a master work, but also to devote all their skill to illuminating that master work, revealing it in its best and clearest light. Robert Alter is a masterful scholar and a critic of exemplary sensitivity and tact who, both as translator and as commentator, has placed himself wholly in the service of the artfulness of the Torah. It is *because* he has been so attentive in his commenting that he can afford to be so daring in his translation, so immune to the "heresy of explanation," so faithful to the literary details of the text that other translators either see as impediments or do not see at all. Conversely, it is his adherence to this specifically literary model of fidelity in representation that leads him into commentary that far exceeds the demands of mere annotation.

The conventions of modern publishing allow Alter to embrace the biblical text only by introductions — to the whole project and to individual books — and by comments at the foot of the page. There are, thankfully, no note numbers, only italicized phrases in the comments indicating the passage being addressed; the biblical text is unmarked, so it is easy to ignore the notes and pursue the narrative when one wishes. But of course the reader discerns the presence of the notes, and when they are long and detailed, cannot resist them. Nor should they be resisted; they're wonderful.

Take, for example, the concluding verses of Exodus 25, which describe — rather unclearly, it must be said — the shape of an ornate lamp stand to be placed in the Tabernacle. Here is how the instructions and the chapter conclude: "And you shall make its seven lamps, and its lamps shall be mounted and give light in front of it, and its tongs and its fire-pans — pure gold. With a talent of pure gold shall it be made together with all these furnishings. And see, and make it by their pattern which you are shown on the mountain."

By preserving the parataxis in a dignified sequence of "ands," and by maintaining the repeated direct address — "you shall" — Alter clearly indicates both the ceremonial character of the Tabernacle's construction and the fact that these laws originate in personal communication from the Lord to Moses. The latter point is, of course, emphasized in the specific reference to the revelation on Mount Sinai, but Alter's translation of all these commandments reveals that the personal dimension never departs from them.

By contrast, the colloquial New Living Translation relates the instructions so laconically and impersonally that you would think Moses had picked up the lampstand at Target: "Make a lampstand of pure, hammered gold. . . . You will need seventy-five pounds of pure gold for the lampstand and its accessories." In his general introduction to the translation, Alter emphasizes the importance of *diction* to the translator of the Torah: The language of biblical narrative, and still more of biblical poetry, is elevated in comparison to daily speech. In a society such as ours, where the same informality of speech reigns on television talk shows, on the floors of the Senate, and in the pulpits of churches, the importance of such differentiation may not seem evident. But Alter makes a convincing case that it was important to the biblical authors.

Moreover, in his commentary Alter shrewdly notes that the reference to Moses' mountaintop vision "reflects an effort to anchor the instructions for the Tabernacle, which look like an independent literary unit, in the narrative context that in effect they disrupt." That is, we are forcibly reminded here of the overarching story — the story of the Lord's careful provision for his covenant people — which the numbing detail of instructions may cause us sometimes to forget.

And this is not an isolated example. Just two chapters later the altar is described in similar terms: "And you shall make poles for the altar, poles of acacia wood and overlay them with bronze. And its poles shall be brought through the rings, and the poles shall be on the two sides of the altar when it is carried. Hollow boarded you shall make it, as He showed you on the mountain, thus they shall do." Here again the reminder of the vision the Lord granted Moses on Sinai — but with an addition, the puzzling shift to the third person: "thus *they* shall do." As Alter's commentary notes, "they" are the Israelites, so that the force of the passage is something like this: "God has so taught Moses how to build the altar, and the people of Israel will carry it accordingly." The King James Version doesn't quite get this, and assumes that that last clause means, "so shall they make it." But most modern translations — even including my favorite one, the recent English Standard Version — simply ignore the clause altogether. (The Tanakh translation renders the clause, "so shall they be made," which inexplicably makes the altar plural.)

It is true that the clause, with its sudden shift of grammatical person, is difficult to construe. But Alter assumes that it is there for a reason, indeed for a literary reason (though here, as is usual in Scripture, the literary serves the theological): It is a reminder of the force and point of the whole narrative that takes Israel from Egyptian captivity to the Promised Land. "Thus they shall do" reminds us that while it is Moses who receives the instructions, they are given — the Ark and Tabernacle are given — for the spiritual health of the people of Israel. Long after the death of Moses, the people will still carry, by those long poles, the altar, along with the other precious objects the Lord reveals to Moses; and when the Ark of the Covenant is taken from them by their enemies, their hearts will be broken; and when the Ark is restored to them, their King, David, will respond by "whirling with all his might before the LORD girt in a linen ephod, . . . leaping and whirling before the LORD." (So Alter gives us the scene in his magnificent rendering of *The David Story*.) So that one clause, so neglected by most translators, opens us to an expanse of covenant history that goes beyond even the great bulk of the Pentateuch. Who are "they"? "They" are, simply, Israel.

It is this Israel — a single nation persisting somehow across all the centuries, personified in the name of its father, the striver-with-God first known as Jacob — to whom Moses speaks in the first chapters of Deuteronomy. Alter rightly stresses the peculiarity of this speech. The generation of Israelites who came into the wilderness was judged faithless by the Lord because they were afraid to claim the land that the Lord had prepared for them. They heeded (so we are told in the book of

Numbers) the ten timid spies rather than Joshua and Caleb, the bold ones who were ready to risk all to enter the land of milk and honey. They therefore must continue wandering until they die in the wilderness, so that almost everyone Moses addresses in his great homily is under the age of twenty. Yet, Alter notes,

> Moses repeatedly speaks as though they were all direct participants in or observers of the episodes he mentions. There is, I would say, a slide of identification between one generation and another. Most of those listening to Moses' words could not literally have seen the things of which he speaks, but the people is imagined as a continuous entity, bearing responsibility through historical time as a collective moral agent. It is this assumption that underwrites the hortatory flourish, repeated in several variations, "Not with our fathers did the LORD seal this covenant, but with us — we that are here today, all of us alive."

This is truly an extraordinary claim by Moses, because in a very obvious sense it *was* the fathers of his audience with whom God had sealed his covenant. But the obvious sense is not, here, the correct one. Moses is teaching the young people before him that the covenant is renewed in every generation: Every generation *is* Israel, as fully as Moses is, as fully as Jacob himself was.

Alter, as a reader mindful of artfulness, is constantly alert to the ways the Pentateuch subtly incorporates the grand story of Israel into the details of the text — even (or especially) those details that most translators and commentators ignore. And not just details, but even great swaths of text that interpreters tend to read cynically or condescendingly. The excruciatingly specific instructions that we have been considering — given twice, in full — are treated by many modern commentators as evidence that (as Alter put it in his *Art of Biblical Narrative*) "the redactors were in the grip of a kind of manic tribal compulsion, driven again and again to include units of traditional material . . . for reasons they themselves could not have explained"; and by other commentators as evidence of a priestly caste determined to make its own responsibilities and obsessions central to Scripture.

Alter considers such assumptions "ungenerous." He grants that the priestly authors of the Hebrew Bible were doubtless sensitive to "the concerns of their own sacerdotal guild," but he also doubts that so cynically simplistic an explanation for strange textual features is adequate to the complexity of the biblical text. For the devotee of the documentary hypothesis, every puzzling passage is an opportunity to introduce another capital letter (J, E, D, P) denoting another source or another unnamed redactor. But Alter prefers to "assume that the ancient writers and their audience had different ideas [than ours] about literary unity and about how story related to law." This leads him consistently to make the charitable presumption that the biblical authors knew what they were doing, which in turn allows him to exert his considerable critical skills to imagine what that might have been.

The result is a translation-and-commentary that indeed shows the unfamiliar and often unexpected literary excellence of the Pentateuch. And because Alter (unlike Kierkegaard's Christian scholars) has no interest in "protecting" us from the biblical text, his work also, however unwittingly, provides devotional encouragement to one who would read this text "religiously." Reading the edgy, rhythmical prose of Alter's translation, and consulting his tactful but richly woven commentary, such a reader comes away with a deepened sense of the providential care of the Lord for his Israel, the minute particularity of the covenantal relationship initiated by this God who allows not a sparrow to fall but by his will and numbers the very hairs of our heads. Has a story ever been at once so comprehensive, so intricate, and so integral as the one Alter gives us here? One is tempted to call it inspired.

A Religion for Atheists

ALAIN DE BOTTON has been engaged for many years now in an intriguing project: to get people to think of philosophy not as an abstruse academic discipline but rather as a guide to living. He has written several books in which he brings the resources of philosophical reflection to bear on topics that matter to everyday people: love, travel, happiness, the buildings in which we live. And now, writing in a new and quite interesting British magazine called *Standpoint,* de Botton takes up the topic of religion.

His opening move is to declare his boredom with the current conversation on the topic, his sense of its "banality." The problem, as de Botton sees it, is that one particular issue regarding religion "has hogged the limelight," and that's the question of "whether or not the whole thing is 'true.'" Now, one might naturally protest that whether religion, or some religion, is true is precisely the question up for debate, but de Botton is having none of that. No, he says, "We'd be wiser to start with the common-sense observation that, of course, no part of religion is true in the sense of being God-given. There is naturally no holy ghost, spirit, *Geist,* or divine emanation." And, helpfully, he adds that "dissenters from this line can comfortably stop reading here."

Now, this is somewhat puzzling, in that in the first paragraph of his essay de Botton had written that his boredom with the topic of religion encompassed both "a hardcore group of fanatical believers" and "an equally small band of fanatical atheists." But in saying that "common

23

sense" is enough to determine that religions — all of them, presumably — are "of course" simply and wholly false regarding their primary characteristics, hasn't de Botton wholly identified himself with those atheists? How does his dogmatism on the matter differ from what he calls their "fanaticism"?

Heck if I know. But de Botton wants to portray himself as a mediating figure, and on these grounds: He thinks there are elements of religious practice, though not religious belief, that are important to people's well-being and that atheists should not ignore. He then proposes — and this is the title of his essay — "A Religion for Atheists." So, what does this religion consist of?

For one thing, cathedrals. De Botton likes cathedrals a lot, and he thinks there should be more of them. "Imagine a network of secular churches, vast high spaces in which to escape from the hubbub of modern society and in which to focus on all that is beyond us. . . . We begin to feel small inside a cathedral and recognize the debt that sanity owes to such a feeling." Presumably, existing cathedrals — little enough used in de Botton's native Europe — can't be repurposed, as we like to say these days, in service of this project because of their historical associations and the art within them, which so relentlessly emphasizes the transcendent. But is that really a problem? After all, there are many man-made structures available to make us feel small: the Sears Tower, Hoover Dam. De Botton, who lives in London, could just take a train down to the Millennium Dome, which in his scheme could finally find a proper use.

But this would be pointless, because it is not the purpose of cathedrals simply to make people feel small (there is no virtue in feeling small) but rather to help people understand that they are located within the vast orderly architecture of creation. We are indeed small, but a small part of something glorious, in which we can participate, find our place, find our purpose. Cathedrals are celebrations of all that God has made, and they embody in their stone and glass the history of God's dealings with his world and people made in his image. If we want merely to feel small, it is enough — though it is increasingly difficult — to find a place away from cities where we can observe the night sky and its stars.

Aside from generating a sense of smallness, de Botton's secular religion would do two other things: It would "use all the tools of art in order to create an effective kind of propaganda in the name of kindness and virtue," and it would "try to counter the optimistic tenor of modern society and return us to the great pessimistic undercurrents found in traditional faiths."

Here we are in more interesting territory, but, to explain why, we need to back up and take note of another comment made by de Botton. "In the early, euphoric days of the French Revolution," he writes, "the painter Jacques-Louis David unveiled what he termed 'A Religion of Mankind,' a secularized version of Christianity which aimed to build upon the best aspects of the old, discredited tenets. In this new secular religion, there would be feast days, wedding ceremonies, revered figures (secularized saints), and even atheistic churches and temples. The new religion would rely on art and philosophy but put them to overtly didactic ends: It would use the panoply of techniques known to traditional religions (buildings, great books, seminaries) to try to make us good according to the sanest and most advanced understanding of the word."

De Botton concludes this section of his essay by admitting, with an evident sigh, that "unfortunately, David's experiment never gathered force and was quietly ditched, but it remains a striking moment in history." Interestingly, de Botton doesn't choose to point out that David's Religion of Mankind was ditched by the leaders of the revolution because it was insufficiently dedicated to *la Patrie*. De Botton commends David for imagining "what a religion might look like if it didn't have a god in it," but that's just what the revolutionaries did too. They went on to create their own secular religion focused on the glory of France, transforming the just-completed church of Sainte-Genevieve into the Pantheon, a temple dedicated to the great men of the country. Voltaire and Rousseau were even disinterred from their burial places and reinterred there — *pour encourager les autres,* one might say.

David's Religion of Mankind, says de Botton, is "a naive yet intelligent attempt to confront the thought that there are certain needs in us that can never be satisfied by art, family, work, or the state alone." But history, and not just the history of the French Revolution (think of Nazi

Germany, the Soviet Union, communist China), suggests that, when people imagine a religion without a god, the state simply becomes that god. And from the French Revolution on, these governments expended great energy, time, and money "to try to make us good" — through propaganda, yes, but also through more rigorous means when propaganda didn't do the job.

Though de Botton does not openly acknowledge this point, he knows it, which is why he sandwiches his propaganda program with two strategies of constraint: the intimidating presence of the secular cathedrals and the catechesis in pessimism. De Botton understands that profound optimism about human nature and the exercise of power — what used to be called hubris — led earlier repudiators of God and the Church to build their secular religions in ways that encouraged the most horrific abuses imaginable.

De Botton's caution and constraint in this matter are commendable. I do, however, have one final set of questions for him. Who's going to build these cathedrals? Where's the money going to come from? Who will determine the content of the virtue-building propaganda? Who will establish the proper degree of pessimism, so the visitors to the cathedrals will not be thrown into despair? I sense, as I peer into the distance, yet another bureaucratic unit of the European Union arising, like Venus from the sea.

Bran Flakes and Harmless Drudges

I

IN 1952 Maria Moliner seems to have grown bored. She and her husband had moved to Madrid some years before, from Valencia, to educate their children. But the children were mostly grown now, Maria's husband was often away, and her work as a librarian provided little stimulation. Moliner (born in 1900) had been one of the few Spanish women of her time to take a university degree, in history, and though it was an honors degree an academic position was unthinkable: even as a librarian she suffered from suspicion, prejudice, and a dearth of intellectual challenges. So she passed the time by returning to her deepest intellectual love, linguistics and lexicography. She decided that she would produce, all by herself, a dictionary: a complete dictionary of the Spanish language as it was actually used.

To some degree this task constituted a protest — a protest against the work of the official guardians of the Spanish language, the Real Academia Español. These days the RAE's chief production is simply called the *Diccionario de la lengua espanola,* but at the founding of the august body, in 1713, its members worked on what they came to call the *Diccionario de autoridades:* the Authorities' Dictionary. The task of these Authorities was to preserve good Castilian Spanish, to purge it of impurities and unnecessary accretions, and to send it along to the next generation in a pristine state. But, Maria Moliner wondered, what about

27

preserving a record of Spanish as it was actually *used?* It was not a *Diccionario de Autoridades* she wished to produce but rather a *Diccionario del uso del español* — so she titled *her* project.

She expected the work would take her two years. Instead it took fifteen, and it's a miracle that it didn't take far longer than that, especially when you consider that the Authorities of the first Academia labored over their project for fourteen. But in 1966 and 1967, the two volumes of Maria Moliner's *Diccionario del uso del español* appeared, weighing about seven pounds and comprising more than three thousand pages. The Colombian novelist Gabriel García Marquez, writing in 1982, gleefully noted that Moliner's dictionary was more than twice the size of the RAE's, which he thought appropriate, since in his judgment it was "more than twice as good."

2

Two hundred and six years before Maria Moliner thought to assuage her ennui by dictionary-making, Samuel Johnson, a rather obscure and not especially successful writer, was approached in his London rooms by a publisher named Robert Dodsley. Dodsley wanted Johnson to make a dictionary of the English language. Many years later Johnson would tell his friend James Boswell that he "had long thought" of such a task before Dodsley approached him. This is probably true. But then, Johnson thought of many tasks, and even took detailed notes about them in his journals; he never lacked for ideas. Summoning the resolve and discipline to carry them out was his problem. For decades he chastised himself for "Idleness" and prayed that God would grant him the power overcome it. Yet he also, famously, affirmed that "No man but a blockhead ever wrote, except for money." (Maria Moliner would have been incomprehensible to him.) Fortunately for Johnson and the English language, Dodsley offered money.

Robert Dodsley, like many British intellectuals of his time, worried that English, that great and noble language, lacked — well, lacked something like an Authorities' Dictionary. In the matter of national lexicographical discipline, the English were running well behind their Continental neighbors. The Real Academia Español was itself a relative latecomer to the dictionary-making, language-fixing game, having been preceded by the Académie français (founded by the great Cardinal Richelieu in 1635) and the oddly named Accademia della Crusca (originating in Florence way back in 1582). In Italian "crusca" means bran: these Florentine scholars called themselves *la Crusconi* — the bran flakes — in reference to their task of separating the linguistic wheat from the chaff, which is what all such academies seem to want to do.

But in England no such body had ever managed to generate itself, though the Royal Society — that great scientific organization, founded in 1660, whose early members included Christopher Wren, Robert Boyle, Robert Hooke, and John Locke — had set as one of its earliest tasks the formation of "a committee for improving the language." One member of that committee was the reigning Poet Laureate of England, John Dryden, and it is interesting to note that one of his chief concerns was a tendency to "corrupt our English Idiom by mixing it too much with French." (This mirrors today's obsession, in the Académie francais, with the elimination of "Franglais," that is, the appropriation of English words by French speakers. In this matter I sympathize with the Académie, since the widespread use of terms like "le parking" and "le weekend" threatens to make the entire nation sound like Pépe le Pew.)

The Royal Society's committee soon disbanded, however, without producing anything, and for the next fifty years or more some of the major English writers would lament the absence of a true British "Academy" to prevent, or at least control, linguistic abuse. For Daniel Defoe, the chief pestilence was lewd, rude slang — "Vomit of the Brain," he called it; for Jonathan Swift it was the fashionable cant of "illiterate Court Fops, half-witted Poets, and University Boys." In the face of such abuses, Swift thought, the only remedy was to discover "some method . . . for *ascertaining* and *fixing* our language for ever." This is a recurrent theme among linguistic academicians and their allies: a deep conviction that the dominant usage of their own time — or, more precisely, the usage into which they were educated, the usage of their youth and young adulthood — is a pure or ideal form of the language, any deviation from which marks a decline.

But no British Academy was formed, and though dictionaries of one kind or another had been produced in England almost since the invention of the printing press, by the time Dodsley came to Johnson, it seemed clear that none of them met the perceived need. This was largely because such dictionaries tended to focus on specialized topics, or were simple lists of words to facilitate more regularity of spelling, or were explanations of particularly difficult words only. (Thus William Tyndale once hoped to add a glossary of unusual words to his translation of the New Testament, though he did not live long enough to do so.) As Henry Hitchings points out, "in the very year that Johnson began his task, [the bishop and literary scholar] William Warburton was still mournfully reflecting . . . 'We have neither Grammar nor Dictionary, neither Chart nor Compass, to guide us through this wide sea of words.'"

A good bit of the history I have just recounted is found in Hitchings's new book, *Dr. Johnson's Dictionary: The Extraordinary Story of the Book that Defined the World.* It's a delightful and informative book, despite its subtitle. (Hyperbolic and extended subtitles are all the rage in publishing these days: see also Mark Kurlansky's *Cod: A Biography of the Fish That Changed the World,* or Thomas Cahill's *The Gifts of the Jews: How a Tribe of Desert Nomads Changed the Way Everyone Thinks and Feels.* It's a trend that can't end too soon.) Hitchings describes the making of Johnson's dictionary, examines its character, and charts its future influence, all with real skill.

For Johnson indeed accepted Dodsley's commission — primarily for the money, of course, though no doubt the honor he could bring his country and its language was an additional incentive. Johnsonians have long debated whether Johnson ever meant for his dictionary to be a truly prescriptive one; but at the outset of his task, in 1747, he wrote a lengthy "Plan" for his dictionary which he addressed to the Earl of Chesterfield, whose patronage he hoped to secure, and early in his account he says quite clearly that the goal of his dictionary is "to preserve the purity and ascertain the meaning of our English idiom." Moreover, he returns to this claim as he concludes his Plan: "This, my Lord, is my idea of an English dictionary, a dictionary by which the pronunciation of our language may be fixed, and its attainment facilitated; by which its purity may be preserved, its use ascertained, and its duration lengthened."

No Academy could have put it better. Yet elsewhere in the Plan, Johnson confesses to some nervousness about being put in such a position of determinative authority, and in effect says that he wouldn't even attempt it if the earl did not so desire. For the earl — this much is crystal-clear — would never have supported Johnson's work if he had not thought that it would rout bad usage and enthrone excellence of style and diction. He said as much in several essays that he wrote while Johnson was at work.

Despite Chesterfield's insistence, during his labors on the dictionary Johnson became more and more uneasy about its usefulness as a prescriptive bludgeon. His principles on this matter may have evolved; or he may have been simply overwhelmed by the magnitude of the task he was facing. He had hired, near the beginning, six assistants, whose primary task was to organize the great piles of lexicographical material that Johnson amassed in his daily reading. For this was Johnson's chief work: to read. Though he was already known (by those who knew him at all) as a vastly learned man, he read hundreds and hundreds of books during the dictionary-making years — sending the assistants out to buy or borrow more whenever his stock ran low — and made notes on every usage that seemed to him unusual or illustrative, or for that matter morally compelling. Johnson thought that good linguistic usage also comprised sage counsel, and wanted his dictionary to be a repository of wisdom as well as literary skill. He wanted the quotations he selected to be useful not simply for "conveying some elegance of language," but also, at least in many instances, for offering "some precept of prudence or piety." Few other than Johnson would ever have imagined dictionary-reading as a school for virtue.

Johnson's decision to employ quotations from skilled and wise writers in most of his definitions was perhaps his most fateful one. It certainly committed him irrevocably to one of the world's great reading projects; and it would set an example to be followed most famously by the *Oxford English Dictionary.* Moreover, it's almost certain that the breadth of his reading contributed to his increasing discomfort with prescription. By the time he wrote his great and justly famous Preface to the completed work, he was ready to state straightforwardly that his goal was not to "form" but to "register" the language. Surely this change of purpose had something to do with the vast diversity of use and meaning that he discovered in his reading. To take but one example, Johnson discerns 65 distinct meanings of the verb "to fall," 63 of which he illustrates with quotations. No wonder he would later admit that many of his early ideas were "the dreams of a poet doomed at last to wake a lexicographer."

And no wonder he almost quit the task a dozen times in frustration or exhaustion or both. The booksellers who sponsored the project wanted Johnson to work more quickly, and were reluctant to advance him the money he needed to pay his assistants; the assistants themselves tended to be incompetent or dishonest or both. "I do not know how to manage," he wrote, plaintively, to one of the more sympathetic booksellers. The misery of those years find their way into the closing words of his Preface:

> Though no book was ever spared out of tenderness to the authour, and the world is little solicitous to know whence proceeded the faults of that which it condemns; yet it may gratify curiosity to inform it, that the *English Dictionary* was written with little assistance of the learned, and without any patronage of the great; not in the soft obscurities of retirement, or under the shelter of academick bowers, but amidst inconvenience and distraction, in sickness and in sorrow: . . . I may surely be contented without the praise of perfection, which, if I could obtain, in this gloom of solitude, what would it avail me? I have protracted my work till most of those whom I wished to please, have sunk into the grave, and success and miscarriage are empty sounds: I therefore dismiss it with frigid tranquillity, having little to fear or hope from censure or from praise.

Indeed he had suffered much in those years, from the failure of his tragedy *Irene* and the death of his wife Hetty as well as from stress and poverty and his habitually deep depressions, which were exacerbated by all of the above. It is rather odd to hear such a lament expressed so forthrightly in the preface to a dictionary, of all things; but such openness is characteristic of Johnson, who was anything but the Olympian figure often evoked by his honorific titles ("Doctor Johnson," "Great Cham of Literature") and perhaps also by the stateliness of his prose. His own suffering always served to make him more attentive to the suffering of others; thus the constant parade of dirty, needy people into his household, his patience and care for whom annoyed his more scrupulous friends. His sympathies were engaged in the same way and to the same degree by language: in the great edition of Shakespeare that he prepared some years after completing the *Dictionary,* he wrote, "I was many years ago so shocked by Cordelia's death, that I know not whether I ever endured to read again the last scenes of the play till I undertook to revise them as an editor." No one has ever been more sensitive to the manifold powers of words than Johnson, and though this is not commonly regarded as a qualification for lexicographical work, that may be unfortunate.

Johnson's uniquely strong personality — "no man can be said to put you in mind of Johnson," a friend said upon his death — finds its way into the very sinews of the *Dictionary* itself. As Hitchings rightly notes, and as Paul Fussell noted before him, Johnson quite self-consciously affirmed that he was "writing" rather than merely "compiling" a dictionary, working with the same intensity of feeling and vision that went into his poems and essays. His personality is woven into the texture of the book, in ways both trivial and deeply serious. The wry definition of "lexicographer" — "a harmless drudge" — is a famous example, as is his definition of "oats": "a grain, which in England is generally given to horses, but in Scotland supports the people." (This is almost universally thought to indicate Johnson's contempt for the Scots, and it is true that he held no high opinion of them; but Johnson felt deeply for all in poverty, and it has always seemed to me that the definition arose from pity rather than scorn.) He could be politically opinionated, defining "excise" as "a hateful tax levied upon commodities, and adjudged not by the common judges of property, but wretches hired by those to whom excise is paid"; he could be literarily opinionated, defining "sonnet" as "a short poem consisting of fourteen lines . . . not very suitable to the English language"; and sometimes he could be just plain exasperated: "to worm" is "to deprive a dog of something, nobody knows what, under his tongue, which is said to prevent him, nobody knows why, from running mad."

In addition to telling us much about Johnson's procedures and practices in the making of the dictionary, Hitchings also gives us a reliable and entertaining guide to its reception. At first there was considerable doubt about the project; Sir Horace Walpole, convinced that no dictionary produced by a single person could ever be successful, wrote, "I cannot imagine that Dr. Johnson's reputation will be very lasting"; and the dictionary, and Johnson himself, suffered violent attack in the book *Lexiphanes,* written by one Archibald "Horrible" Campbell, whom Hitchings describes as "a ship's purser of apparently fabulous ugliness." Johnson's use of contemporary quotations, even from periodicals, aroused the strong disapproval of the more particular. (Curiously, this scene would be repeated 130 years later, when Benjamin Jowett — the Master of Balliol College, a dominant figure of late-Victorian Oxford, and the head of a university committee overseeing the ongoing work of the *OED* — forbade the editor, James Murray, from using newspaper quotations to illustrate meanings. Murray protested heatedly against such interference and in the end won his independence: the newspaper citations stayed.) But the *Dictionary* received, surprisingly, an early commendation from the *Crusconi* of Florence — that is, the Accademia della Crusca — and grew in stature as the years went by. One can get a sense of just how dominant a cultural force it became by reading the first chapter of Thackeray's *Vanity Fair:* "the Lexicographer's name was always on the lips" of Miss Pinkerton, headmistress of a girls' school, and his *Dictionary* is described as "the interesting work which she invariably presented to her scholars, on their departure" from her institution. When Becky Sharp receives hers — at the moment she is leaving — she immediately throws it out the window of her coach.

But some years later the makers of the *OED,* differing strongly from Becky on this point as on most others, used 1,700 of Johnson's definitions with little or no change. And at the outset of our new millennium, 17 members of the U.S. Congress brought a lawsuit against then-President Clinton for his failing to obtain from Congress a declaration of war before ordering airstrikes against Slobodan Milosovic's Yugoslavia. After all, does not the Constitution specifically grant to Congress the power to declare war? But that simply raised the question of what the word "war" means — and in order to find out what it might have meant to the authors of the Constitution, the District of Columbia's U.S. Circuit Court of Appeals, before which the case was argued, saw fit to consult what would have been *the* lexicographical authority of their time: Samuel Johnson's *Dictionary*. What they discovered is written into the court records: "War may be defined [as] the exercise of violence under sovereign command against withstanders; force, authority and resistance being the essential parts thereof. Violence, limited by authority, is sufficiently distinguished from robbery, and like outrages; yet consisting in relation towards others, it necessarily requires a supposition of resistance, whereby the force of war becomes different from the violence inflicted upon slaves or yielding malefactors."

3

Twenty years before Johnson began his dictionary, a lexicographer named Benjamin Martin wrote:

> The pretence of fixing a standard to the purity and perfection of any language is utterly vain and impertinent, because no language as depending on arbitrary use and custom, can ever be permanently the same, but will always be in a mutable and fluctuating state; and what is deem'd polite and elegant in one age, may be counted uncouth and barbarous in another.

These words should make the epitaph of all Academies of language, and all forms of classicism as well — meaning by *classicism* what C. S. Lewis calls "the curious conception of the 'classical' period of a language, the correct or normative period before which all was immature or archaic and after which all was decadent." Lewis devotes several pages of the long and magnificent introduction to his history of 16th-century English literature to a learned disembowelment of the classicist ideal. The Renaissance humanists (in Lewis's account the first classicists) "succeeded in killing the medieval Latin" in which so much great poetry and prose was written; "before they had ceased talking of a rebirth it became evident that they had really built a tomb." Once scholars "vied with one another in smelling out and condemning 'unclassical' words . . . the permitted language grew steadily poorer" and ultimately unable to represent or even grapple with the changing world of things and events. (One humanist even "bound himself by oath to abstain not only from every word but from every number and case of a word that could not be found in Cicero.") Lewis is right to say that the great flowering of English literature at the end of the 16th century — Sidney, Spenser, Shakespeare, Donne — is something the classicists would have prevented if they had had the power.

This is not to say that there are no excellences or barbarities in language. There are both, as Lewis well knew. But this grasping at past excellences as a means of preventing future barbarities is a mug's game. To steal a line from William F. Buckley, Jr., there are certainly times to stand athwart history yelling Stop, but not in the linguistic arena; yelling there is "utterly vain and impertinent." In some periods linguistic change will accelerate, often because the world to which language must respond is itself changing, and while such cultural instability can be disorienting, it is also often the source of great linguistic creativity. Some linguistic horrors were perpetrated in the heterogeneous and unstable world of Shakespeare — but then Shakespeare too was perpetrated then. There is much to be said for the view of Noah Webster, the great American successor to Johnson: Webster certainly believed in preserving the purity of the English language — indeed he felt that in England the language had by his time become far more degraded than in North America — but he also believed that one of the key responsibilities of the lexicographer was to record and enshrine valuable new usage.

This could be called an American view, I suppose, engaging as it does a confidence in linguistic progress, albeit with a recognition of real degradation and loss; but then Johnson's employment of contemporary quotations suggests that he too believed that new uses of old words could be worthy of commendation. This hopefulness about linguistic change seems to me not so much American as un-Academic: Academies seem, in general, to be far less open to the new than individual lexicographers. In the stories we have explored here, from the original *Crusconi* to today's Académie français, from Samuel Johnson to Maria Moliner, one can trace the Cartesian coordinates of lexicography: on the X axis, the distinction between individual and collective works; on the Y axis, the distinction between descriptive and prescriptive works. And when one does that, one can see that it is usual for there to be a strong correlation between the collectively produced dictionaries and a tendency to prescribe. Through most of the history of dictionary-making it has been thought that dictionaries are supposed to prescribe — that is, teach people how to use the language properly — so it would be surprising if even the lone pilots of lexicography didn't have a tendency to the pedagogical. But, to judge from the examples of Johnson, Webster, and Moliner, they tend to be uneasy about such pedagogy, or flexible about the lessons to be learned, or even dismissive of the whole idea.

Looking at these coordinates, it's also easy to discern on our chart one great outlier: the *Oxford English Dictionary,* or, as it was originally called, *A New English Dictionary on Historical Principles.* For this very reason, surely, it is the greatest of all dictionaries: the product not of a committee of distinguished academics but rather a shockingly motley collection of word nerds and amateur pedants, it prescribes nothing, instead preferring to provide the most exhaustive (but necessarily imperfect and incomplete) accounting possible of the full range of English usage. The *OED* is the world's largest linguistic rummage sale; it would not inspire the devotion it does were it not so vast and *simultaneously* so ragtag. Some years ago the physician and writer Oliver Sacks bought a photocopier for the sole purpose of copying pages from the bulky *OED* to read in bed; this story alone has reconciled me to the invention of that otherwise loathsome machine. For the *OED* is the most complete representation yet devised of language itself.

Even the most prescriptive dictionary, even the strictest Academy, has a different effect than it intends: the sweeping prohibition of a particular word or usage merely reminds the reader of options and alternatives, perhaps previously unsuspected ones. ("This is marvelous," the novelist Stendhal is reported to have said when he tasted ice cream for the first time; "what a pity it isn't forbidden." As with ice cream, so with language.) However, the exhibition of sheer potential embodied in every dictionary only happens, it seems to me, when the dictionary actually has a body. Surely every user of dictionaries or encyclopedias can recall many serendipitous discoveries: as we flip through pages in search of some particular chunk of information, our eyes are snagged by some oddity, some word or phrase or person or place, unlooked-for but all the more irresistible for that. On my way to "serendipity" I trip over "solleret," and discover that those weird, broad metal shoes that I've seen on the feet of armored knights have a name. But this sort of thing never happens to me when I look up a word in an online dictionary. The great blessing of Google is its uncanny skill in finding what you're looking for; the curse is that it so rarely finds any of those lovely odd things you're *not* looking for. For that pleasure, it seems, we need *books*.

This helps to explain, I think, my otherwise curious indifference to the Octavo DVD-ROM edition of Johnson's *Dictionary,* released in commemoration of the book's 250th anniversary. Octavo is a company that takes high-resolution photographs of rare and old books, digitizes them, and sells them on CD or DVD. Medieval illuminated manuscripts, architectural drawings from the Italian Renaissance, painstakingly rendered Victorian paintings of parrots and turtles, even Gutenberg's Bible — all these make themselves vividly present on one's computer screen. But Johnson's *Dictionary* just lies there, splayed like a patient etherised upon a table, or a specimen readied for dissection. It can't be browsed or thumbed, its pages can't be ruffled; you can't practice the *sortes* upon it, closing your eyes and stabbing a finger down on a spot to discover what lesson God or chance has left there for you. If you want to find anything the only reasonable way to do it is by typing text into a search window à la Google. I use Google as often as the next guy, and praise it more than most; but it makes me sad to see Johnson's wonderful book, made "amidst inconvenience and distraction, in sickness and in sorrow," digitized into lifelessness.

George Landow has written that "the linear habits of thought associated with print technology often force us to think in particular ways that require narrowness, decontextualization, and intellectual attenuation, if not downright impoverishment." But it turns out that, when it comes to dictionaries anyway, it's hypertext that narrows and impoverishes. The simple fact that I cannot pick up a dictionary and turn to the precise page I wish, or, even if I could do that, focus my eyes only on the one definition I was looking for — the very *crudity*, as it were, of the technology is what enriches me and opens my world to possibilities. Only when I hold the printed book can I be ushered into the world of sheer fascination with proliferating language that people like Maria Moliner and Samuel Johnson inhabited, and encourage us to inhabit.

Before that dark conclusion of his Preface, Johnson allows us some insight into the delight that, often at least, punctuated his "harmless drudgery." Perhaps he began his project with hopes of prescribing and regulating the language, but he soon enough learned what he was in for: "words are hourly shifting in their relations, and can no more be ascertained in a dictionary, than a grove, in the agitation of a storm, can be accurately delineated from its picture in the water." It would be wrong to hear this as a lament; Johnson is rather confessing his awe at the ordinary vastness, the day-to-day sublimity, of the hoard of words our ancestors have gathered over the centuries of English. Looking back at his labors, before remembering the losses he incurred during them, he wrote, "I saw that one enquiry only gave occasion to another, that book referred to book, that to search was not always to find, and to find was not always to be informed; and that thus to persue perfection, was, like the first inhabitants of Arcadia, to chace the sun, which, when they had reached the hill where he seemed to rest, was still beheld at the same distance from them."

On the Recent Publication of
Kahlil Gibran's Collected Works

I

Expansive and yet vacuous is the prose of Kahlil Gibran,
And weary grows the mind doomed to read it.
The hours of my penance lengthen,
The penance established for me by the editor of this magazine,
And those hours may be numbered as the sands of the desert.
And for each of them Kahlil Gibran has prepared
Another ornamental phrase,
Another faux-Biblical cadence,
Another affirmation proverbial in its intent
But alas! lacking the moral substance,
The peasant shrewdness, of the true proverb.

O Book, O *Collected Works of Kahlil Gibran,*
Published by Everyman's Library on a dark day,
I lift you from the Earth to which I recently flung you
When my wrath grew too mighty for me,
I lift you from the Earth,
Noticing once more your annoying heft,
And thanking God — though such thanks are sinful —
That Kahlil Gibran died in New York in 1931
At the age of forty-eight,

So that he could write no more words,
So that this Book would not be yet larger than it is.
O Book —
To return to my point,
Which I had misplaced in my wrath —
O Book,
Five times I open you at random,
Five times I record for my readers what I see.

At the first opening, these words:
"And I gazed at Him, and my soul quivered within me,
        for He was beautiful."

At the second opening, these words:
"You the talkative I have loved, saying, 'Life hath much to say';
        and you the dumb I have loved, whispering to myself,
        'Says he not in silence what I would fain hear in words?'"

At the third opening, these words:
"Work is love made visible."
To which I reply, You must have been pretty lucky in your job,
If you ever actually had a job,
But then I recall myself to myself,
And I discern that my task at the moment is but to open the book,
Not to comment thereupon.

Therefore I turn, and cause the Book to be opened a fourth time:
"Men do not desire blessedness upon their lips, nor truth
        in their bowels"
— And I make no comment about the bowels,
But rather allow the completion of the thought, such as it is —
"For blessedness is the daughter of tears, and truth is
        but the son of pain."

And therefore the fifth and thank God the last
Opening of the Book is at hand:

"Absolve me from things of pomp and state,
For the earth in its all is my land,
And all mankind my countrymen."

Five times I have opened the Book,
And here I swear a great vow that I opened truly at random,
Except that once I opened to a narrative passage
That, had I quoted it, would not have made sense.

Not that any of the rest made sense either,
But you, my reader — you know what I mean.

II

In the twenty-third year of the twentieth century,
Alfred A. Knopf published *The Prophet,*
Written by this Kahlil Gibran,
And lo, the copies of it that have been bought
Would fill the granaries and storehouses of Lebanon,
From whence the Author came to this country as a child.
Even now, these many decades later,
In the great marketplace of Amazon,
The sales rank of *The Prophet* is high,
Higher at this moment than any of my books has ever been,
Except one of them, once, fleetingly,
And at that thought I gnash my teeth
And once more fling the Book to the Earth.

But wise is the author who can master the rage of jealousy,
And the mastery thereof is peace;
So I calm the spirit within me and ask,
What desert of human desire is watered by Gibran's oases,
The Prophet above all, but also *The Garden of the Prophet*
And *Jesus the Son of Man* and *Spirits Rebellious*
And poems and sketches numerous and miscellaneous?

Wherefore do readers turn to these books,
And what do they find within them that nourishes and comforts?

Let it be known, first, that the lands of the West
Treasure up in their hearts images of Araby.
In the time of the great Queen known as Victoria
There arose in England a race of men
Whose delight was in the desert,
Who dreamed of Scheherazade and her tales of Haroun-al-Raschid,
The greatest of the Caliphs, the master of disguise,
Who glided half-hidden through the markets and alleys of Baghdad.
Sir Richard Burton found English words to tell of him.
Likewise did Edward Fitzgerald give unto us many
      Englished quatrains
Of the *Rubaiyat* of Omar Khayyam, that old Persian
Whose heart found its twin in dark-minded Koheleth:
'Tis all a Chequer-board of Nights and Days
Where Destiny with Men for Pieces plays:
Hither and thither moves, and mates, and slays,
And one by one back in the Closet lays.
The Moving Finger writes; and, having writ,
Moves on: nor all thy Piety nor Wit
Shall lure it back to cancel half a Line,
Nor all thy Tears wash out a Word of it.

So spoke Fitzgerald's Persian bard,
And the people of Victoria heard him and sighed,
And thought unto themselves "Vanity of vanities, all is vanity,"
And turned again to contemplate, now sad, their railway
      timetables.

To these who loved their Orient, their Persian Araby
(For in England and America those two lands seemed one),
Gibran came with a double portion, yea a triple.
He poured it out without stint
And oft, it seems, without editing.

This is the first cause of his great renown.
And the second is like unto it: Gibran's Jesus,
An oriental sage, a speaker of wry Wisdom,
A lover of paradox, a Judge only of others —
Oh yes, He can be wrathful,
But never to me the reader of Gibran,
Only to those whom I already dislike,
The powerful, the greedy, the cruel:
Those with whom I shall never be confused.
(The family Gibran was Maronite Catholic,
And in this faith Kahlil was raised,
And though he loathed the Church
He claimed always to love Jesus.
But the truth of this claim I cannot tell.)

To me — and perhaps to you, dear sisters and brothers —
The Jesus given by Kahlil Gibran, and likewise his Prophet,
Who is himself somewhat Jesusish, bring words of comfort:
What befalls us is part of the plan.
But no — I repent me of some lowercase letters —
I mean to say, Part of the Plan.

The Prophet teaches us to rest and to accept.
The Prophet teaches us that our desire for Freedom binds us,
That our aversion to Pain hurts us,
That we foolishly seek Knowledge because we do not Know
        that we already Know,
Or something like that.
But how this Wisdom shall comfort those whom disease afflicts,
Or who rot in prison,
Or who grow faint with hunger,
That too I cannot tell.
Yet surely the Prophet speaks well and wisely.

That the Prophet delights in paradox
I need not say.

If he contradicts himself, he contradicts himself,
But in so doing illuminates us all the more.
The Prophet warns,
"Say not, 'I have found the truth,' but rather, 'I have found a truth,'"
One of infinitely many truths, it seems,
"For the soul walks upon all paths,"
Which means that anything the Prophet says
Falls like a perfectly formed olive leaf
Upon at least one of those paths,
So that His profundity is everlasting and without diminishment,
As long as he pronounces oratorically
After the manner of Sir Laurence Olivier
Reading the King James Bible.

And it is the voice of Sir Laurence
Reading the King James Bible
That I hear within me as I write these words,
Which echo resonates within and bequeaths to me
The Prophetic Strain,
At least as far as you know.
Once that voice enters the mind,
As it does when one has read hundreds and hundreds of pages
　　　of Kahlil Gibran,
Its abode is fixed within,
It refuses all notices of eviction,
It continues to loop within the sphere of one's skull,
An earworm, dread and implacable.

III

Envy me not, then,
O my friends, my readers;
Though the Prophetic Strain echoes in each line I write,
Though you covet said Strain for your own,
Heed me and flee.

The words I give you now are words of Life, and not Death,
Though I suppose the Prophet would proclaim that
Death and Life are the same,
And that only the foolish would divide the two,
The Two which are One.
But He'd be wrong about that, I'm pretty sure.
So again I turn and I say to you,
Pass by the *Collected Works of Kahlil Gibran,*
Touch it not nor gaze upon it,
But go about your ways in peace of heart and with thanksgiving.
Fly, you fools!

The Poet's Prose

POETS HAVE rarely found their calling lucrative. The occasional fortunate one finds a patron to keep him — yes, "him": almost no female poets have found patrons — in wine and cigarettes, and some, from Sidney to Byron to James Merrill, have benefited from the inheritance of title or cash. (Merrill's father co-founded Merrill Lynch.) But the great majority have had to seek profitable work. Matthew Arnold was an inspector of schools, Wallace Stevens an insurance executive, William Carlos Williams a physician. Robert Graves used to say that his novels — *I, Claudius* and so on — were dogs he raised and sold in order to buy food for his beloved cat, Poetry. And of course American society today has achieved a universal solution to the problem of keeping our poets fed, housed, and insured: creative writing programs.

For much of his adult life, W. H. Auden struggled with this problem. Through the 1930s he worked mostly as a schoolmaster in various English public schools, so when he came to America in 1939 (to stay, as it turned out), one of his major concerns was to find a job. Aside from a brief teaching stint at the University of Michigan, soon after his arrival, and a longer period (1942-44) at Swarthmore College, that work turned out to be writing for periodicals: *The New York Times Book Review, The Nation, Commonweal, The New Republic, The Saturday Review, Harper's,* even — this shows how truly omnipresent the man was — *Mademoiselle.* Writing in 1955 from the island of Ischia, in the Bay of Naples, Auden would say that "the winter months" — which he spent in New

York — "are those in which I earn enough dollars to allow me to live here in the summer and devote myself to the unprofitable occupation of writing poetry."

But those multitudinous essays and reviews served another and perhaps more noble purpose. Auden had decided to stay in America largely because the country offered him a respite and refuge from his own English reputation: as the Thirties had worn on, Auden had become increasingly uncomfortable with his role as "voice of a generation," and had come to see that those who most admired him had the strongest and most fixed ideas of what he should write. Living in America offered him the opportunity to take some deep breaths and reassess his own intellectual and poetic equipment: he read astonishingly widely, and his writing for periodicals gave him the opportunity to marshal his thoughts and place his reading within a framework of his own needs and interests.

Out of this re-imagining of himself came Auden's embrace, sometime in 1940, of the Christian faith in which he had been raised. But if his spiritual awakening was in some sense a result of his reading and thinking, it also prompted a great deal of further reading and thinking, as he tried to reconcile what he knew of Christianity with what he knew of the modern world. That task would occupy much of his prose in the decade following his arrival in America. One could say that in that decade Auden built for himself a vast and rambling, but architecturally coherent, intellectual house. And for the rest of his life he would inhabit that house. Its making is admirably chronicled in *The Complete Works of W. H. Auden: Prose, Volume II: 1939-1948,* which appeared in 2002, as edited by the literary executor of Auden's estate, Edward Mendelson — who also happens to be Auden's best critic. And now Mendelson has given us the next volume in the series, which covers Auden's essays, reviews, and miscellaneous writings from 1949 to 1955. Astonishingly, this is a significantly larger volume than the previous one — 779 pages to 556 — even though it covers less time; and it contains many of Auden's most ambitious and significant critical writings. If the previous volume chronicled the construction of Auden's intellectual domicile, this one contains, scattered throughout its pages, not only pretty thorough renovation of the building but also a major treatise on architecture.

There are of course dozens of appreciations of individual books and authors here too, including ongoing assessments of Freud — who had long been a figure of totemic significance for Auden — and a glowing review for *The New York Times Book Review* of a curious book called *The Fellowship of the Ring.* (Auden would later review *The Return of the King* for the same periodical and with equal enthusiasm. He was the first figure of unquestionable cultural authority to celebrate Tolkien, whose lectures on Anglo-Saxon Auden had attended as an Oxford undergraduate, an experience that had a lasting and powerful effect on his own poetry. Tolkien was very grateful for Auden's interventions on his behalf.) But these appreciations are not at the heart of the book. What we find within these pages is the fullest picture available of how the mature Auden came to understand his role as a poet — and especially a poet who was also a Christian.

Editorial introductions to volumes like this one are rarely the source of much instruction, and almost never do they bring delight, but Mendelson's introductions to each of the five installments so far of Auden's *Complete Works* have been unfailingly elegant and magisterial. The current one sets the scene by noting that the volume begins with Auden's first book of literary criticism, *The Enchaféd Flood,* which marked the culmination of Auden's work in the previous decade and brought that project to a kind of conclusion. If one figure can be seen as presiding over that period in Auden's life, it is certainly Kierkegaard — whose American reputation Auden did a great deal to promote — but at the end of *The Enchaféd Flood* Auden utters a kind of valediction to the Kierkegaardian world: the individual mind, bedeviled by anxiety, working out its salvation in fear, trembling, and terrifying isolation. That world was, in many respects, Auden's own in his first American years, as he sought to remake himself with few sympathetic friends to share the journey. But now (writing in 1949) he sees himself and his society as entering a new era.

This new era is fundamentally social and communal: the anxious individual must now enter into fellowship with others, and must be willing to submit to public order and public truth: "the necessity of dogma is once more recognised," Auden wrote, "not as the contradiction of reason and feeling but as their ground and foundation." That self-contained, self-accountable figure of Romantic and modernist myth, the "fabulous voyager" (to borrow a phrase from Joyce) whose bold independence was seen as the sole source of great human achievement, must now give way: in our suddenly post-Kierkegaardian age "the heroic image is not the nomad wanderer through the desert or over the ocean, but the less exciting figure of the builder, who renews the ruined walls of the city."

Auden had been thinking seriously about the relationship between art and community since the beginning of his career, and had come up with a kind of position paper in 1940 in his remarkable long poem "New Year Letter," but this was on the cusp of his conversion, and at the outset of what would prove to be a catastrophic world war. His vision of community at that time was small, local, nearly private. But throughout the rest of that decade, he devoted a great deal of mental energy to contemplating the possibilities of a more public order after Christendom, whose destruction he believed to be complete. One of the most important books for Auden in those years was Charles Norris Cochrane's great *Christianity and Classical Culture,* which describes the founding of the Constantinian project, and it is helpful to imagine Auden, with Cochrane's work echoing in his mind, traveling to a devastated Germany in 1945 to interview German civilians for the U.S. Strategic Bombing Survey. "The ruined walls of the city" indeed.

Auden was decades ahead of most other Christian intellectuals in his thinking about community, about Christendom, about the complexities of citizenship and public life for Christians in a post-Constantinian world; and few of those who have caught up with his interests have been able to match the nuances of his thought. As Mendelson shows us, in the period represented by this volume of prose, Auden came to believe that these difficult issues can only be seriously approached after one has made an elementary but vital distinction between nature and history. The uniqueness of human beings, in the created order, is that we live simultaneously in nature (the realm of involuntary and repetitive acts) and history (the realm in which we make choices, and experience and reflect upon the consequences of those choices). Other living things — plants and other animals — live in nature only; angels, perhaps, only in history. To have this double inheritance is our challenge, our pain, but also our glory. Thus, in one of his finest poems of the 1950s, Auden writes, "Woken at sun-up to hear / A cock pronouncing himself himself / Though all his sons had been castrated and eaten, / I was glad I could be unhappy" — because to be unhappy is to experience the dignity of history, the gift of understanding that what I feel is at least in part the result of acts (mine and those of other human beings) that were chosen, not mandated by instinct or tossed into the world by accident, what Thomas Hardy called "crass Casualty."

Auden always argued that few could match Kierkegaard's acuity of insight into the historical (choice-driven) aspect of human experience. But he came to believe that for Kierkegaard — and many who succeeded him, "bowled over" by his brilliance as Auden had been — our life in nature is at best an embarrassment. (With perhaps pardonable exaggeration, Auden remarked of Kierkegaard that one "could read through the whole of his voluminous works without discovering that human beings are not ghosts but have bodies of flesh and blood.") And for Auden this deficiency is properly described as theological: Kierkegaard, and other Christian thinkers who share his disregard for embodied human nature, neglect clear and vital Christian teaching about God's redeeming love for this physical world, this whole Creation.

Much later in his life, Auden would borrow a musical metaphor from Dietrich Bonhoeffer and say that Kierkegaard was a "monodist, who can hear with particular acuteness one theme in the New Testament — in his case, the theme of suffering and self-sacrifice — but is deaf to its rich polyphony." And for the Auden who emerges in the pages of this volume, the unique power of Christian doctrine is its polyphonic character, its capacity to address every dimension of our being, to give a comprehensive account of how history and nature relate, and — decisively in Christ's incarnation, crucifixion, and resurrection — how they may be reconciled. In a 1955 essay about his conversion — the only straightforward one he ever wrote — he put the main point in this way:

> As a spirit, a conscious person endowed with free will, every man has, through faith and grace, a unique "existential" relation to God, and few since St. Augustine have described this relation

more profoundly than Kierkegaard. But every man has a second relation to God which is neither unique nor existential: as a creature composed of matter, as a biological organism, every man, in common with everything else in the universe, is related by necessity to the God who created that universe and saw that it was good, for the laws of nature to which, whether he likes it or not, he must conform are of divine origin.

And it is with this body, with faith or without it, that all good works are done.

As Mendelson points out in *Later Auden* (1999), the best book anyone has yet written about the poet, it was in 1948 that Auden "began to write poems about the inarticulate human body" — the part of us that does not and cannot talk, or think, or have faith in God, but which Christ died to redeem, along with the rest of creation which, as St. Paul says, groans in anticipation of its deliverance. Cardinal Newman distinguished between "notional" and "real" assent, and while Auden gave notional assent to the physical Resurrection of Jesus, and to the credal claim that "we look for the resurrection of the dead and the life of the world to come," he always struggled to make that assent real. But he understood these affirmations to be absolutely central to orthodox Christianity and necessary to a true embrace of the goodness of Creation.

It is interesting and also slightly comical to see how relentlessly Auden inserts these distinctions into his essays and reviews. His ingenuity in this enterprise is truly remarkable. But this is simply an indication of how vital he thought the distinctions are, and how disastrous the "existentialist" neglect of nature and the human body. Auden was a natural and irrepressible pedagogue, and while he had given up teaching in schools, periodical writing provided ever-new outlets for that side of his character. An introduction to a collection of George MacDonald's writings allows him to develop a theory of Dream Literature; a review of a Dostoevsky travel journal (commissioned and then left unpublished by *The New Yorker,* probably because they thought it was too cranky) turns into a lecture on the virtues of the bourgeoisie too often scorned by intellectuals. Writing on Isaiah Berlin's famous division of intellectuals into hedgehogs and foxes, Auden insists, borrowing from

Lewis Carroll, that they can also be divided into Alices and Mabels. And I was surprised to see how many of the pieces collected here feature Auden explaining Americans to the British or the British to Americans, tasks he always pursued with great energy and sublime confidence.

It was during the years represented in this collection that Auden began to think about putting together a major critical statement, something like his own version of Coleridge's *Biographia Literaria.* It was not Auden's way to put this in the form of a treatise or consecutive argument, but rather as a collection of *pensées,* meditations, reflections. Most of what ultimately went into that book, which Auden would title *The Dyer's Hand,* may be found in one form or another in this new volume. Some of his major lectures — those on Shakespeare that he gave at the New School for Social Research in Manhattan in 1946, those he gave a decade later when he was named Professor of Poetry at his alma mater Oxford — made their way into the book revised but recognizable. But many of the parts of *The Dyer's Hand* are compiled from bits and pieces of the writings collected here: the Alice/Mabel dichotomy is neatly extracted from the discussion and repurposed, along with dozens of self-contained chunks from other essays. Many of these deal in one way or another with the relationship between Christianity and art, which, Auden told Stephen Spender, "is what the whole book is really about, the theme which dictated my selection of pieces and their order." And it's interesting, in light of this half-hidden purpose, to reflect on how much of the book takes the form of notes and aphorisms. It had been Pascal's plan to form his *pensées* into a book with a single strong line of argument, though he did not live to do so; Auden by contrast seems to have waived, or repudiated, such an ambition, contenting himself with more scattered provocations.

This decision was in part a bow to his own temperament and natural inclination, but also in part an awareness that the pace at which he had been working for the previous fifteen years — along with his rather heavy drinking and his pursuit of "the chemical life," the use of amphetamines to get him working in the morning and barbiturates to get him to sleep at night — was wearing him out. This volume concludes with the year 1955, during which Auden turned forty-eight, but he was already beginning to talk of himself as an old man. Three years later he would buy a house, a cottage in an Austrian village near Vienna, and sometimes he would walk into his garden in the morning and weep with gratitude to have a place of his own. Between his arrival in Austria in 1958 and 1964 he would write a lovely sequence of poems about his house, "Thanksgiving for a Habitat," would put together *The Dyer's Hand,* and would (along with Chester Kallmann) produce the astonishing and, alas, utterly unknown libretto for Hans Werner Henze's opera *The Bassarids;* but he wrote nothing major after that. It's fair to say that by his early fifties Auden had effectively completed his life's work. The cottage in Kirchstetten had become something like a place of retirement — like the Sabine farm of the great Roman poet Horace, whose disciple Auden considered himself to be.

This third volume of Auden's prose, then, shows us the poet, the thinker, at the very height of his powers — a height he would not occupy much longer. The six years of miscellaneous writings collected here reveal a mind of prodigious range, curiosity, and synthesizing power; the reader can turn to almost any page at random and discover delights. But we must also remember that he wrote most of these pieces because he had to, and that during this same six-year period he also produced his greatest poetic achievement, and in my judgment the greatest poetic achievement of the twentieth century: his Good Friday sequence, the *Horae Canonicae.* There you will find many of the ideas I have been describing expressed concisely, beautifully, memorably; and there you will find much more. Read these essays; but then read the poems they fed and of which they are, for all their brilliance, a pale shadow.

The Brightest Heaven of Invention

IN OCTOBER of 1954 the poet W. H. Auden reviewed a curious new book for the *New York Times.* The book was written by an Oxford medievalist named Tolkien whose lectures Auden had attended as an undergraduate, and it was called *The Fellowship of the Ring.* Auden liked it very much, and one of his commendations is particularly noteworthy: "The first thing that one asks is that the adventure should be various and exciting; in this respect Mr. Tolkien's invention is unflagging."

Invention — a curious word. Today it is used almost exclusively to refer to *things,* things clever people have come up with. Inventors produce inventions: the transistor, a new insulating material, an "X-Y Position Indicator For A Computer Display System" (commonly known now as a mouse). But there are other meanings of the word with far older provenance, and it might be worth our while to recall them. In ancient rhetoric, for instance, *inventio* is the early stage of composition during which one imagines the arguments that best support one's position. *Inventio* is thinking things up. The young Cicero believed this skill so important that when he wrote a treatise covering almost every aspect of oratory he called it simply *De Inventione.*

In literature "invention" has a slightly but intriguingly different meaning. In his *Defence of Poetry* (1585), Sir Philip Sidney writes that the poet "calleth the sweet Muses to inspire into him a good invention" — that is, asks the Muses to give him wonderful stories to tell. The orator coming up with good arguments is bound to reality, or ought to be;

but, Sidney says, "Only the poet, disdaining to be tied to any such sub-jection, lifted up with the vigour of his own invention, doth grow, in ef-fect, into another nature." In Shakespeare's *Twelfth Night* we find a homely and comical version of the same idea when Toby Belch instructs Andrew Aguecheek to write a note: "It is no matter how witty, so it be eloquent and full of invention."

By "poet" Sidney means the writer of what we would now call "liter-ature," whether in prose or verse. Sidney himself displayed his inven-tion most fully in his long, extravagant pastoral romance, *Arcadia,* in which, over the course of hundreds of pages, dramatic scene succeeds dramatic scene, plots twist and retwist, characters enter and exit and enter again when least expected, more often than not in disguise. When today we study *The Faerie Queene,* by Sidney's great contemporary Spenser, we are likely to puzzle over the allegory and tease out the po-litical and religious contexts and explore the intricacies of the Spenser-ian stanza, but what his contemporaries most valued in him was his in-vention, his apparently endless facility for producing fabulous stories.

These writers exhibit not just excellence of invention, but abun-dance of it — a trait particularly esteemed by Erasmus, who wrote a whole book about it: *De duplici copia verborum ac rerum* (On the Abun-dance of Words and Ideas). This was Erasmus's version of Cicero's trea-tise, in which a single virtue is singled out as exemplary of the whole craft of oratory — and look at the virtue they choose to emphasize. Erasmus likes *copia* so much that at one point in his treatise he lists 150 different ways you could say "Your letter has delighted me very much."

In these matters the model for Spenser and Sidney was the great Italian poet Ariosto, contemporary of Erasmus and author of the *Or-lando Furioso,* which was one of C. S. Lewis's favorite books. It was Ariosto whom Lewis has primarily in mind when he wrote, in the midst of a serious scholarly book, that his "ideal happiness . . . would be to read the Italian epic — to be always convalescent from some small ill-ness and always seated in a window that overlooked the sea, there to read these poems eight hours of each happy day." And yet — to circle back to our beginning — when Lewis wrote his own commendation of *The Lord of the Rings* for the dust jacket he made this claim: "If Ariosto rivalled it in invention (which in fact he does not), he would still lack its heroic seriousness." (Lewis was getting carried away here, and one can scarcely blame Edwin Muir for commenting that "Nothing but a great masterpiece could survive the bombardment of praise directed at it from the blurb.")

Lewis and Auden alike knew, when they commended Tolkien for this virtue, that they were speaking an archaic language, that it had been many years — centuries perhaps — since serious writers were specially celebrated for their invention. In fact, it is pretty safe to say that some decades before Lewis and Auden wrote about Tolkien the term had virtually disappeared from the vocabulary of literary criticism. Why is that?

One reason involves the development of literary criticism as an academic discipline, something that happened in the latter part of the nineteenth century. Before that, reading and reflecting on literature was something that all well-bred persons were expected to do; it was no more to be taught at university than the habit of drinking port after dinner. Those who sought to bring literary study into the university curriculum needed some justification for their field, needed to show that the study of literature is something far more rigorous and objective than the expression of good taste through the encounter with *les belles lettres*. It therefore became necessary for literary study to develop quasi-scientific *methods* of inquiry and to eschew evaluation. The question of whether a poem is good or bad, being a matter of mere taste and not subject to methodological codifying, could safely be left to the poets and book reviewers; scholars had more vital tasks to attend do.

But "invention" is an intrinsically evaluative term: it is a trait that a writer benefits by possessing, or suffers from the lack of. Moreover, no method could determine its presence or absence. It therefore has no clear place in a scholar's vocabulary.

It is also worth noting that the rise of literary scholarship is roughly contemporaneous with the move of the realistic novel to the center of literary experience, and it is not the place of the realistic novel to emphasize invention. The highly inventive writer does not represent everyday reality but rather imagines a new reality, or, to borrow Sidney's phrase, grows into another nature. Of course, the defender of inventive stories would say that in the deepest and truest sense Spenser or Sidney or Ariosto can hold the mirror up to nature — *human* nature — as well as Tolstoy or George Eliot. But they do not do so by following the canons of realistic fiction, and so come to be seen, by certain serious-minded critics anyway, as less than fully serious. There's something undignified and perhaps even irresponsible in cheerfully ignoring probabilities and the furniture of daily life in order to make up stories about winged horses, improbable escapes from the fiercest of prisons, or the miraculous return of crown princes kidnapped as infants and long thought dead.

And — I hope I am not fouling my own scholarly nest by saying this — there is yet another possibility: that invention is not a virtue that scholars hold in high regard because it is not a virtue that they tend to possess. The patient, careful craft of a George Eliot (who is not any less of a genius for the patience and care) is more congenial to the scholarly mind, though Eliot herself could be wickedly critical of a certain kind of scholar.

Writers whose greatest gift is invention *can* become the object of serious critical attention *if* they happen to possess other traits that are more amenable to scholarly ways of thought. Thus my earlier comment that critics have plenty to say about Spenser, who is in no danger of being neglected or undervalued. Similarly, there are matters of politics and technique in certain contemporary authors — Salman Rushdie, say, or Gabriel Garcia Marquez — that give critics plenty to chew on, though they may never get around to noting the fact that those writers are characterized above all else by their profligate invention. Academic scholars have to justify their jobs by writing or talking, and about *The Faerie Queene* or *Midnight's Children* or *One Hundred Years of Solitude* there is a great deal to discuss.

In a recent essay on the contemporary American short story, Michael Chabon commends the story that entertains — implicitly, the story that entertains by its inventiveness. We suspect the entertaining story, he writes, for two reasons. First, the entertaining story produces pleasure, and "it's partly the doubtfulness of pleasure that taints the name of entertainment. Pleasure is unreliable and transient. Pleasure is Lucy with the football. Pleasure is easily synthesized, mass-produced, individually wrapped." And this last sentence leads Chabon to his second explanation for our suspicion of entertainment: its link (in our minds anyway) with passivity, with a one-way street leading from the maker to the receiver of entertainment's pleasures. "The entertainer balloons with a dangerous need for approval, validation, love, and box office; while the one entertained sinks into a passive spectatorship, vacantly munching great big salty handfuls right from the foil bag."

All this leads Chabon to imagine the ideal contemporary fiction writer as a kind of Trickster, a straddler of boundaries, in this case especially that boundary that separates the world of "genre fiction," where *inventio* reigns, from the world of "literary fiction," where we never think to commend a writer for such a virtue, even in the unlikely event that he or she should possess it. (Of course, the first writer likely to come to mind as an example of such a genre-transgressing Trickster is probably Michael Chabon, but his distinctions are useful all the same.) Though he doesn't put it in quite this way, Chabon seems to imagine the Serious Reader as a kind of anti-hedonist, willing to swallow the delightful confections of the entertainingly inventive writer if they are presented with a suitably bitter coating of stark realism (psychological or otherwise).

But what about *The Lord of the Rings,* which possesses the virtue of invention in profligate spades but is notably deficient in most other literary virtues? Tolkien himself did not feel that there was much point in debating the book's merits:

> *The Lord of the Rings*
> Is one of those things;
> If you like it, you do,
> If you don't, then you boo.

A reader will either recognize and value the book's inventive heart or not, and in either case there's not much point in arguing. I sometimes wonder how Tolkien would respond to those critics who have vigorously argued for his inclusion in the scholars' canon because of the way his book functions as a mirror of the Great War, or on the ecocritical grounds that he is a kind of patron saint of environmentalism. I'm inclined to think that he would appreciate the effort but see it as rather beside the point. And I know he would smile at the English journalist who, upon learning that *The Lord of the Rings* had won the Waterstone's bookshop "book of the century poll," muttered, "Oh hell! has it? Oh my God. Dear oh dear. Dear oh dear oh dear."

That journalist was distressed not because Tolkien is an inventive writer but because (in the considered judgment of the British intelligentsia) he is a politically reactionary and racist one. But writers whose primary virtue is invention are not likely to get serious critical attention even if their politics are either invisible or impeccable. Such writers will probably not even present themselves as candidates for the attention of Serious Readers, instead occupying the territory of genre fiction (Patrick O'Brien) or stories for children (J. K. Rowling). Though some of them feel condescended to and can get rather grumpy about that — Stephen King being a notable instance — is such critical neglect really such a lamentable thing? Not every book needs to be appreciated by scholars, and it may be for the best that some much-loved books lie permanently beyond the reach of academic critique.

Meanwhile, as Abraham Lincoln is alleged to have said, "Those who like this sort of thing will find this the sort of thing they like." And I think it likely that among that group a disproportionate number will be Jews and Christians. It is the DNA of the story that has shaped them. The pattern and model of *inventio* is, surely, the first chapter of the book of Genesis. And as for *copia,* it has never been exemplified so grandly as in the great catalogue that the Lord speaks from out of the whirlwind, that celebration of his own profligacy that leaves Job blasted, befuddled, shamed, and yet, somehow, consoled. Those who are Serious Readers of *that* story may perhaps be forgiven for being a little less strict, a little more generous, with others.

Opportunity Costs

THE STAB of envy came instantly, unexpectedly. I was somewhere quite new to me: on one of the enormous ferries that run between the mainland of British Columbia and Vancouver Island. As we moved westward we traded shifting clouds for brilliant morning sunshine. My wife and I had every expectation of a delightful day on the island, and had even managed to procure some surprisingly good coffee from a helpful machine. We sat at a small round table, sipping the coffee and gazing on the small islands in the Strait of Georgia; all was well indeed. But then my eye strayed to a neighboring table. There sat a ten-year-old boy, gazing fixedly upon the face of his father, who was reading in a tense whisper from *Harry Potter and the Half-Blood Prince*. It was July 16, 2005. The book had been released just eight hours earlier, at midnight, and though I had felt a slight pang when I discovered that I would be vacationing in Canada at the time — celebrating my 25th wedding anniversary, as it happened — I dismissed it immediately, and gave the matter no further thought. (Except, that is, to order a copy from Amazon Canada and have it sent to the B&B where we would be staying. With my wife's permission, *of course*.) I had every reason to believe that the book would be waiting for me when we returned that evening, but at the moment that prospect yielded little comfort. (I got still less when the book didn't show up at all. But that's another story.) It occurred to me that this was the first time since the first book in the series that anyone I knew read a Potter installment before I did. When the second one, *Harry Potter and the Chamber of Secrets,* appeared in Britain some months before it was scheduled to appear in the United States, I ordered *that* volume from Amazon U.K. — as did thousands of others, a practice that quickly led Scholastic, J. K. Rowling's American publisher, to insist upon simultaneous release of future volumes. From then on I read each book on the day of its publication, and even wrote an essay in praise of J. K. Rowling (one that received much critical commentary from my Christian brothers and sisters).

Why this excitement? Why would a middle-aged man — who also happens to be a professor of literature — get so worked up about a series of books for young people? Indeed, why do so many millions of people get similarly worked up, as they have about no other books? There is no real answer to this question, though every time another book in the series is released the newspapers of the world fill with speculations. The closest we can come to an answer is to note that J. K. Rowling does three things exceptionally well: first, she creates characters readers really care about — not just Harry but also Ron, Hermione, Hagrid, Dumbledore, Neville, etc. — usually because they possess some admirable trait (kindness, or courage, or wisdom) but are also somehow vulnerable; second, she writes suspenseful plots, so that you really want to know how it's all going to come out; and third, she creates a whole imaginative world that people love to inhabit, even after they already know what happens in the stories. Many writers can do one of those things; a few can do two; hardly any can achieve all three. (Tolkien is one of them, which is why he also, though a very different and much greater writer than Rowling, is equally beloved.) It's the combination that makes her special.

Critics who complain that Rowling's writing style is pedestrian or cliché-laden — Harold Bloom being prominent among them — therefore miss the point. She is certainly not much of a stylist, she does indeed fall sometimes into cliché, and in fact a key moment in the new volume, one meant to be deeply moving, is marred by the kind of grammatical error that makes an English teacher like me grind his teeth and mutter about the decline in the professional skills of editors. But the last thing I want when I'm reading a Harry Potter book is to pause and admire the felicity of the diction. This ain't Emily Dickinson, after all.

And I found that grammatically erroneous passage deeply moving anyway because I cared about the characters involved, I cared about the story, I cared about the world.

That world — let's start there — has been a source of great delight to me over the years. Rowling's imaginative universe takes every dusty old piece of furniture from the common stock of tales about witches — pointed hats and cloaks, flying broomsticks, eye of newt and toe of frog, the whole shebang — cheerfully accepts it, and raises it to the next power. She adds to that the love of odd names that also characterized Charles Dickens, matching his Dick Swiveller with her own Argus Filch, and his town of Eatanswill with her village of Hogsmeade. It is tempting to heap up examples. She has a keen ear for the absurd, and has picked up curious words and phrases from all over the place: the names of two of her main characters, Dumbledore and Hagrid, seem to have been taken from a passage about country dialects in Thomas Hardy's *Mayor of Casterbridge.* (A "dumbledore" is a bumblebee, and to be "hagrid" is to be worn out.) The portraits at Hogwarts School of Witchcraft and Wizardry talk, and the subject of any one will occasionally depart to visit the inhabitants of the others; in the great wizard shopping street called Diagon Alley one can buy Self-Stirring Cauldrons; rooms and tents and even automobiles are often bewitched so that their insides are larger than their outsides. Each book in the series has added to this storehouse of treasures and curiosities.

But *Harry Potter and the Half-Blood Prince* does so less than any of its predecessors. Such new information about the magical world that we acquire is disturbing if not terrifying: we learn, for instance, of the Horcrux, an object enchanted to receive a portion of a person's soul — but only when that person has severed a bit of his soul by murdering someone. One of the few light-hearted moments in the book comes early on, when Harry and his friends visit Weasleys' Wizard Wheezes, the joke shop run by Fred and George Weasley, and see a variety of magical pranks and tricks. But one of the new comical items Fred and George are proud of — Peruvian Instant Darkness Powder — much later in the book enables one of Harry's enemies to escape capture, and this escape leads, indirectly at least, to the death of a beloved character. There is no less magic in this book than in any of the others, but any distinction between serious and frivolous magic is being occluded, or even erased.

So too is the distinction between "good" and "dark" magic — or, as the magicians of the Renaissance would have put it, between *magia* and *goetia*. In the previous installment of the series, *Harry Potter and the Order of the Phoenix*, a group of students wants to learn how to defend themselves against possible attacks by Dark wizards, especially the Death Eaters, the most trusted servants of the greatest and Darkest of Dark wizards, Lord Voldemort, Harry's great antagonist. They are all taking a course called Defense Against the Dark Arts, but it is useless, so they determine to study under the tutelage of Harry, who by this time has had to defend himself against the Dark Arts more than a few times. Harry's dear friend Hermione Granger invents a way to inform people of future meetings: she enchants coins so that their serial numbers are replaced by the date and time of the next meeting of the Defense Association. Clever indeed! But the same enemy who buys Peruvian Instant Darkness Powder from Weasleys' Wizard Wheezes learns of the trick and employs it to bring Death Eaters into Hogwarts Castle. Moreover, the meetings of the Defense Association take place in a place called the Room of Requirement, which alters its shape, size, and furnishings in order to meet the needs of the people using it; and this room is also commandeered by Harry's enemy, again following our heroes' example.

These are sobering events that require some reflection. In Harry Potter's world, magic does not involve communing with spirits. (The contrast with the recent Bartimaeus books of Jonathan Stroud — in which the *only* power that wizards have is the power to summon and command spirits — is noteworthy.) Rowling has imagined magic as a kind of technology, but one that works only for some people. And even those people have to study and practice to be able to use the technology correctly: learning to use a wand is not so different from learning to drive a car. Like many of the technologies we are familiar with in our Muggle world, magical ones tend to be morally neutral: insofar as they have power, that power can be used for good or evil, and the greater the power, the greater its effect in either direction. So one is tempted to say that what Hermione designed for good purposes was taken by a Dark wizard and used for evil ones; but such a judgment would be too facile.

Yes, Dolores Umbridge — the Defense Against the Dark Arts teacher who, in her other capacity as High Inquisitor of Hogwarts, prohibited secret meetings — is a nasty piece of work; and yes, though she is not a Dark wizard herself, her policies aid and abet the forces of Darkness, and inhibit the ability of good wizards to combat those forces. Hermione's little invention would seem, then, perfectly justified in the troubling circumstances; and at the time no one questions it. But here at the end of the next volume we see it in a new light: we are reminded that, after all, it was a device to ensure secrecy, to prevent the faculty and staff of the school from learning what some students were up to. And when the school is led by Albus Dumbledore rather than Dolores Umbridge, the success of such deception becomes disturbing.

Yet it must be said — and this too is a reflection prompted only by the concluding chapters of book 6 — that Dumbledore himself has not only tolerated deception by Harry and his friends, he has positively encouraged it. Key to many of Harry's secret adventures is the Invisibility Cloak that he inherited from his father — but it was actually given to him by Dumbledore, and once when Harry had lost it, Dumbledore returned it to him. Near the end of *Chamber of Secrets,* Dumbledore acknowledges that Harry has "a certain disregard for the rules," but he does so with a twinkle in his eye — even though he makes this comment in listing the traits prized by Salazar Slytherin, the ancestor (literally or figuratively) of the Dark wizards that plague the wizarding world in these books. Rowling raises the possibility here that Dumbledore's encouragement of deceptive practices by his most gifted and devoted students has been a significant mistake.

If so, it would not be his only one. In the latter pages of *Order of the Phoenix* Dumbledore confesses that he had withheld important information from Harry — information about the link between Harry and Lord Voldemort — for several years. He says that he did so out of concern and affection for Harry. But in fact secrecy seems to be habitual with Dumbledore. In a recent interview, Rowling made this intriguing comment: Dumbledore's "wisdom has isolated him . . . where is his equal, where is his confidante, where is his partner? He has none of those things." By the time book 6 begins, Dumbledore has recognized this problem, because he immediately begins taking Harry deeper and deeper into his confidence, trusting him more fully and even relying on him. Indeed, one of the most moving passages in the entire series occurs at a crucial moment in this book, when Harry is trying to help a Dumbledore weakened by powerful Dark magic: "It's going to be all right, sir . . . Don't worry," Harry says. "I am not worried, Harry," the great wizard replies. "I am with you."

But by the time I put down *Harry Potter and the Half-Blood Prince* — rather hag-rid from the excitement and pain of it all — I wondered if Dumbledore had not learned his lesson too late. In the course of the book he reveals much to Harry, but when he has the chance to answer a question that has been of obsessive concern to Harry, and to many other characters, since the first book in the series, he refrains:

> "Professor . . . how can you be sure Snape's on our side?"
> Dumbledore did not speak for a moment; he looked as though he was trying to make up his mind about something. At last he said, "I am sure. I trust Severus Snape completely."

But why, Professor, why do you so completely trust Severus Snape? That question, along with many others, most of them less consequential, will be answered in the final volume, which Rowling has said she will not begin serious work on until next year. Therefore fans of the series will have plenty of time to reflect on the disastrous (or apparently disastrous) events of book 6, and to speculate on possible ways the story could be brought to conclusion.

I find myself thinking especially of something I have already mentioned: the draining away of delight from the books, the narrowing of Harry's horizons to a point, that point being an ultimate encounter with Lord Voldemort. At this stage in the series — the last book could of course surprise me — it is hard to imagine that there will be much room in Harry's mind for any other thoughts. Earlier, when the threats were less immediate, when Harry could be confident in the protection of others, and when he had not yet learned of the depth and strength of his perverse bond with Voldemort, he could revel in the distractions of Quidditch, the wizard sport at which he excels; but Rowling has already said that we have seen a Quidditch match for the last time. In book 6 the only real refuge from war with the Dark Lord is found in adolescent romance; and that, while often funny, is never felt by those who experience it as light-hearted pleasure.

More dismaying is the book's suggestion that Harry (and therefore the story) may not return to Hogwarts at all. Now, I strongly suspect that it will be necessary for Harry to return to Hogwarts in one way or another — he needs to return to the Room of Requirement, I think, and there may be some relics of the Hogwarts founders that he should investigate — but if he did not, there would be a great gaping hole at the heart of the book, because Hogwarts has been a key character in the books, almost as central to the series as Harry himself. In any case, that such a suggestion can even be made indicates the seriousness of the crisis that has come upon Harry and the whole wizarding world. Everything is expendable except struggle with the Dark Lord; and everything that pleases us can be used by the forces of evil for their own purposes.

This foreclosure of possibilities for Harry, the narrowing of his world to a single dreadful task, is an exaggerated and intensified version of what growing up is for everyone. As Robert Nozick once wrote, "Although [young people] would agree, if they thought about it, that they will realize only some of the (feasible) possibilities before them, none of these various possibilities is yet excluded in their minds. The young live in each of the futures open to them . . . Economists speak of the opportunity cost of something as the value of the best alternative forgone for it. For adults, strangely, the opportunity cost of our lives appears to us to be the value of all the foregone alternatives summed together, not merely the best other one. When all the possibilities were yet still before us, it felt as if we would do them all." The "opportunity cost," for Harry and for many others, of defeating Voldemort is terrifyingly high. Handled in a certain way, the denouement of this story could confirm every child's worst suspicions of what it means to grow up.

But I do not think that Joanne Rowling wants to say that adulthood consists in forgoing all delight, all leisure and playfulness, and that young people had better get used to it. Rather, she is showing that there are times when some people, at least, must forgo such pleasures so that they may be retained, or regained, by others. And it is at this point that the comparisons between Rowling's books and *The Lord of the Rings* —

comparisons that I have tended to dismiss — begin to ring true. Reading the last pages of *Harry Potter and the Half-Blood Prince,* I found myself hearing in my head some of the last words Frodo utters to Sam: "I tried to save the Shire, and it has been saved, but not for me. It must often be so, Sam, when things are in danger: some one has to give them up, lose them, so that others may keep them." Harry has indeed given up many things: all the delights of Rowling's imaginative world that I have mentioned, and many more. We are left to wonder whether he must give them up permanently, or whether, his quest complete, he will remain whole enough to reclaim them.

Four people very dear to Harry have died trying to protect him from Lord Voldemort, and at the end of book 6 he is determined that no others shall do so. From this point on he will move forward alone: he ruthlessly, if regretfully, cuts as many ties as he can. But — here again we are reminded of Tolkien, of the refusal of Merry and Pippin and (above all) Sam to abandon Frodo — Ron and Hermione make their position clear: "We're with you whatever happens." I expect that the final book of the series will pay proper homage to the first one, in which the skills of all three friends were necessary to prevent Voldemort from claiming the Philosopher's Stone and thereby achieving endless life. Which is another way of saying that I believe that Voldemort will, in the end, be defeated.

But what will be the cost of victory, to Harry and to those he loves? I am not confident that Harry, Ron, and Hermione will all survive the seventh book. But even if they do, I wonder what the *agon* will do to them. I especially wonder what will be left of the Harry Potter we first met almost a decade ago. Let us meditate on this: in each of the two most recent books in the series, Harry has tried to use an Unforgivable Curse, each time on a person whom he has great reason to hate. Yet he has been unable to perform the curses, because his heart is not in them, his will is not fully behind them. "You need to *mean* them, Potter," says one enemy; "You need to really want to cause pain — to enjoy it." "No Unforgivable Curses from you, Potter!" says the other of Harry's intended victims. "You haven't got the nerve or the ability." Harry, for all the misery and loss he has suffered — perhaps *because* of all the misery and loss he has suffered — finds it impossible to summon and will true hatred. Without that will, without that hatred, will he be able to do what he knows he must do: kill Voldemort? It seems unlikely. But would a Harry who can summon the hatred to kill, even if the Dark Lord himself is the victim, still be the Harry Potter we have come to love?

In the early books in the series — indeed up through the fifth book — the obvious and recurrent historical analogue to the story is the beginning of World War II: the Minister of Magic, Cornelius Fudge, is a Neville Chamberlain figure, an appeaser, in denial about the real state of affairs even though all the evidence is right before his eyes; while Dumbledore (in a kind of "political wilderness" at Hogwarts) is the clear-eyed, straight-talking Churchill of the tale. But the sixth book treats life, not in conditions of open battlefield warfare or air assault, but under the constant but unpredictable threat of terrorism. Thus the debate at the end of the book about whether Hogwarts should remain open: some want it closed to protect the students, while others argue that the students would be safer at Hogwarts than at home, and in any case, they say, the supporters of Voldemort must not be given the satisfaction of knowing that they had closed the school. (This strongly resembles the debates that go on in, say, Israel — though Israelis seem almost fully to have chosen the second option, opting for at least the semblance of normalcy no matter what.)

Rowling denies conscious reference to the current historical moment, and indeed her description of this new wizards' war seems mandated by the intrinsic shape of the story — by the necessary form of Voldemort's rebellion. Still, the first chapter of this book is rather eerie: Cornelius Fudge and his successor show up in the office of the Muggle Prime Minister, who is troubled by a series of strange and destructive events. When he learns that these are not accidents or natural disasters, but rather the work of Voldemort and his Death Eaters, he splutters, "But for heaven's sake — you're *wizards*! You can do *magic*! Surely you can sort out — well — *anything*." To this Cornelius Fudge, with a wan smile, replies, "The trouble is, the other side can do magic too, Prime Minister." (Rowling held a midnight book-release party at Edinburgh Castle on July 16, and had originally planned to read this chapter to the children whom she had invited; but the then-recent Underground bombings in London caused her to decide instead on a chapter from an earlier book.)

Therefore, the great question facing readers who look forward to the seventh and last Harry Potter book is not just which *side* will win, but which *magic* will triumph. Dumbledore has always fought Voldemort through overt and covert action — again, his honesty and courage counter Fudge's head-in-the-sand befuddlement — but he has refused to fight on Voldemort's terms, always refraining from Dark magic (like the Unforgivable Curses). But the effectiveness of that noble refusal now seems to have been called into question. As Harry moves towards his final confrontation with Voldemort, he, by contrast, seems determined to use the weapons of evil against evil. But what does it profit a man to defeat the Dark Lord but lose his soul?

The Youngest Brother's Tale

A LITTLE MORE than a hundred years ago, a number of British educators, journalists, and intellectuals grew exercised about the reading habits of the nation's children. The particular target of their disapproval was the boy's adventure story — the kind of cheap short novel, full of exotic locations and narrow escapes from mortal peril and false friends and unexpected acts of heroism, that had come to be known as the "penny dreadful." Surely it could not be good for children to immerse themselves in these ill-made fictional worlds, with their formulaic plots and purple prose; surely we should insist that they learn to savor finer fare.

Then came riding into the fray a young man — twenty-five at the time — named Gilbert Keith Chesterton, who, though a journalist and an intellectual himself, repudiated the hand-wringing of his colleagues and planted his flag quite firmly in the camp of the penny dreadfuls: "There is no class of vulgar publications about which there is, to my mind, more utterly ridiculous exaggeration and misconception than the current boys' literature of the lowest stratum." Chesterton is perfectly happy to acknowledge that these books are not in the commendatory sense "literature," because "the simple need for some kind of ideal world in which fictitious persons play an unhampered part is infinitely deeper and older than the rules of good art, and much more important. Every one of us in childhood has constructed such an invisible dramatis personae, but it never occurred to our nurses to correct the composition by careful comparison with Balzac."

Nor should our nurses have done so, because what matters most about the penny dreadfuls is the soundness and accuracy of their moral compass, and their power of inspiring their readers to discern the significance of moral choice:

> The vast mass of humanity, with their vast mass of idle books and idle words, have never doubted and never will doubt that courage is splendid, that fidelity is noble, that distressed ladies should be rescued, and vanquished enemies spared. . . . The average man or boy writes daily in these great gaudy diaries of his soul, which we call Penny Dreadfuls, a plainer and better gospel than any of those iridescent ethical paradoxes that the fashionable change as often as their bonnets.

And above all, what Chesterton loves about the penny dreadful is this: "It is always on the side of life."

I have been meditating on these thoughts in recent days, as I have scanned cyberspace for the many and varying responses to *Harry Potter and the Deathly Hallows,* the final tale of the Boy Who Lived. It is a story full of exotic locations and narrow escapes from mortal peril and false friends and unexpected acts of heroism; it is a story which suggests that courage is splendid and fidelity noble. Of course, that's not enough for some people; and for others it's precisely the problem.

We already know that some Christians mistrust the Potter series because of its depictions of magic; we already know that some critics (Harold Bloom most prominent among them) deplore the books' lack of literary grace. But another and different set of critics has emerged here at the end of the series, for whom the evident traditionalism of the books is their greatest flaw. One of the participants in Slate.com's Book Club thinks that the novel, and its epilogue in particular, "feels awfully bourgeois in its concern with little other than our heroes' marriages and children." (I did not know that concern for marriage and children was the exclusive province of the bourgeoisie; but that's why I read Slate, to learn stuff like that.) And as I scanned the blogs I lost track of the number of people who complained that the epilogue, and indeed the whole series, is defaced by "heteronormativity." Not a gay or lesbian couple in sight — though, if it makes anyone feel better, I have seen that a few readers of the previous book, *Harry Potter and the Half-Blood Prince,* think that Harry's obsession with finding out what Draco Malfoy is up to marks a welcome homoerotic interlude.

What could one say in defense of these books, so unliterary, so unsophisticated in their morality and style, so bourgeois, so heteronormative? Perhaps only this: that J. K. Rowling has produced, in the vast, seven-book, thirty-five-hundred-page arc of Harry's story, the greatest penny dreadful ever written.

Chesterton is among the ablest defenders not just of penny dreadfuls but also of the fantastic imagination more generally: "The things I believed most [in childhood]," he wrote a few years after defending the boys' stories, "the things I believe most now, are the things called fairy tales. They seem to me to be the entirely reasonable things. They are not fantasies: compared with them other things are fantastic." But of course such books can also defend themselves. As George Orwell once noted, poems and stories defend themselves best of all simply by surviving; but it is also the case that works of fantasy can openly consider and debate their own terms, their own way of truthtelling. Think of how Sam Gamgee, in Tolkien's *Lord of the Rings,* pauses at times to ask what sort of story he and Frodo are in, and how it might later be narrated. Or that moment early in the book when Boromir expresses skepticism about the information he has received from Gandalf and others: "But what I have heard seems to me for the most part old wives' tales, such as we tell to our children" — to which Celeborn replies, "Do not despise the lore that has come down from distant years; for oft it may chance that old wives keep in memory word of things that once were needful for the wise to know."

There are moments like this in *Harry Potter and the Deathly Hallows.* About a quarter of the way into the story we discover that Albus Dumbledore, the old headmaster of Hogwarts School of Witchcraft and Wizardry whose murder was the shocking culmination of the sixth book, has made provisions in his will for Harry and his two best friends. To Harry he gives the Golden Snitch from the first game of Quidditch Harry ever played; Ron gets a little device that puts out lights, called a Deluminator. These gifts are more than they seem to be, of course, but it's Hermione's gift that's particularly intriguing. Not surprisingly, since Hermione is an obsessive reader and haunter of libraries, her gift is a book; but it's not a guide to advanced magic, or the kind of historical or scholarly study that she delights in. Rather, it's a collection of children's stories, *The Tales of Beedle the Bard,* the wizarding world's equivalent of Aesop's Fables or the Mother Goose tales.

This is strange, and neither Hermione nor her friends know what to make of it; had Dumbledore lacked the foresight to give her a copy in the original ancient runic script — which she must use her scholarly expertise to read and translate — Hermione might have set the book aside altogether. And somewhat later on, when Harry begins to think that one of Beedle's stories, "The Tale of the Three Brothers," might be essential to the quest they are pursuing, Hermione is incredulous. Perhaps she has reason to be incredulous, given that the only person they know who takes "The Tale of the Three Brothers" seriously — who believes it to be historically founded — is one Xenophilius Lovegood, best known in these books for his obsessive pursuit of a purely imaginary beast called the Crumple-Horned Snorkack.

"Xenophilius" means "strange-lover," not incidentally, and the funny thing about the truly strange is that sometimes it's real. "The Tale of the Three Brothers" proves to be pretty much what Mr. Lovegood thinks it is, though, being like most of us foolish and greedy, he completely misunderstands the tale's meaning; and in the event we see that this little story contains not only vital clues for Harry but also a message which, had the evil Voldemort been able to read and profit from it, could well have saved the lives of many, and even saved the Dark Lord's own soul. But Voldemort has no time for fairy stories, old wives' tales: they are childish, they are primitive, they offer nothing to the man who seeks to go farther than any wizard ever has in conquering death.

Had he paused in his career of violence and vengeance to read "The Tale of the Three Brothers" — the very idea is of course absurd — Voldemort would have been interested to note the presence in that tale of a certain object of magical power, an object which obsesses him in this final book in much the same way that the immortality-granting Philosopher's Stone did in the series' first installment. But would he have been able to see and understand what Beedle's little story teaches about that object, about other like talismans, and about death? Of course not. "That which Voldemort does not value," says a wise but deeply flawed man late in this book, "he takes no trouble to comprehend. Of house-elves and children's tales, of love, loyalty, and innocence, Voldemort knows and understands nothing. *Nothing.*" Having discerned to his own satisfaction what magic is worth knowing and what books are worth reading, the Dark Lord strides with absolute confidence towards the end of his own story, an end prefigured in Beedle's little tale. For he is surely the double of that tale's eldest brother, whose younger siblings find their counterparts in this book also.

The key theme of the whole series is the opposition of death and love: the devastation wrought by those whose fear of death causes them to shun love as a weakness, and, in contrast, the rich rewards in store for those who will not allow the fear of death to block love, who know that love risks all for the beloved. Preceding the events of the first book are the sacrificial deaths of James Potter, in a vain attempt to save his wife and son, and of Lily Potter, in an equally vain attempt to save Harry. In the fourth book of the series the deaths resume: Cedric Diggory in that one, Sirius Black in the next, Albus Dumbledore in the sixth. In this final installment the named dead exceed a dozen, and many more remain unnamed. Among those whom Harry knows and cares for, all of them, in this book and in the previous ones, die for someone they love, or for something they believe in.

Though romantic love appears in these books, its role is relatively small: the three chief objects of love in the series are family, friends, and school.

It may seem odd to put school on the same level as family and friends, but there is no question that Hogwarts School of Witchcraft and Wizardry is as central to these stories as Harry Potter himself. J. K. Rowling sees that school — a school like Hogwarts, anyway — can be loved not as an alternative to friends and family but rather as a means of solidifying and clarifying one's love of friends and family. In these books, children who pass through the barrier at Platform Nine and Three-Quarters and board the Hogwarts Express are indeed in some sense leaving their family, and that not only is frightening for them but is also, for their parents, "like a little bereavement" — so we are reminded on the final page of this book. But those parents had also attended Hogwarts, and their characters had been formed there, so we can also say that by sending their children to Hogwarts they strengthen bonds among the family's members.

This fusing of the "school story" with deep commitments to friendship and the integrity of loving families is only possible in the context of that peculiar institution, the British boarding school. It's true that there are still a few Americans who stay in one place long enough to send their children to the same primary and high schools that they themselves attended; and it's true that many more delight in sending their children to the universities from which they themselves graduated. But it's the upper-class British practice of having very young children — Hogwarts brings them in at age eleven — attend school far away from home that creates the unique combination of fear, anxiety, the conquest of fear and anxiety, pride, independence, and nostalgia that we see raised to maximum pitch at Hogwarts.

Likewise, the intensity of life at Hogwarts — and the experience is indeed intense, even in times of peace and calm — means that the friendships formed there are of particular intimacy. This is a note struck in the first book, when certain peculiar circumstances lead Harry and his friend Ron to cooperate with that annoying little know-it-all Hermione Granger. ("There are some things you can't share without ending up liking each other, and knocking out a twelve-foot mountain troll is one of them.")

At Hogwarts, then, the challenges of boarding-school life are multiplied, several times over, by the fact that it is a school of witchcraft. In the world Rowling has created, witchcraft is very powerful and therefore very susceptible to going astray. Leaving aside the dangers generated directly by the Dark Lord and his minions, Harry breaks an arm and (later) fractures his skull playing Quidditch, Ron has his leg snapped by the bite of a giant hound, Neville breaks his wrist falling off his broom, Hermione gets accidentally transformed into a kind of cat person, countless students find themselves burned or otherwise disfigured by potions gone awry or jinxes well-delivered, and so on. Some of Rowling's most creepily delightful inventions concern the patients at St Mungo's Hospital for Magical Maladies and Injuries; and the experience of Luna Lovegood, whose mother died when a spell she was casting backfired, is not unusual. Many of these problems are fixed with relative ease, but even so, the wizarding world is one in which disease, injury, and death seem to be around every corner.

I think that's one of the reasons people find this world so fascinating: our culture is so deeply risk-averse, so determined to punish anyone who might cause injury to us or our children, or even might fail to take precautions to prevent us from being injured, that we can scarcely imagine an environment in which risk is so blithely accepted and injuries dealt with so matter-of-factly. But it is just because Hogwarts is a place which allows young people to take such risks — and therefore to test themselves and grow in capability and confidence — that its students and graduates love it so much. Harry's story culminates in a great Battle of Hogwarts in which people who love the school return to it to fight for it. But they are not the only participants: the figures in the school's many portraits cheer them on, wizards animate the suits of armor that normally stand in the hallways and rush them clanking into the fray, and — in a moment comical but also oddly touching — Professor McGonagall cries "Charge!" and leads a platoon of galloping classroom desks to confront the school's enemies. Hogwarts is fighting for its own life.

Despite their acceptance of risk, wizards feel the threat and misery of death as we do. Molly Weasley is the character who most often reminds us of this: having lost brothers to Voldemort's Death Eaters in the first stage of the war, she is continually fearful for her children, desperate to shield them from danger. But she cannot shield them, and it has been clear for several books now that not all of them — she has seven — are likely to survive to the end.

What happens to people when they die? Wizards don't seem to know much about that. One of the curious things about this fictional world is its complete lack of religious teaching: God is not mentioned in any of the books, except in an exclamation or two ("Thank God!"). So when the young Harry starts to think about this question, he doesn't really know where to turn. The first book in the series tells of a man with the power to make himself immortal who chooses to die instead, and when Harry is surprised to hear this, Dumbledore tells him that "To the well-organized mind, death is but the next great adventure." Throughout the series that idea — it is Dumbledore's governing princi- ple — is repeatedly opposed to Voldemort's belief that death is the worst thing imaginable and that it must therefore be mastered, "eaten."

Harry is not wholly satisfied by the little that his headmaster says on this subject; plus, things keep happening which cause Harry to question Dumbledore's insistence that the dead are fully beyond this world and cannot return to it. In the fifth book Harry even interrogates the Hog- warts ghost, Nearly Headless Nick, only to discover that ghosts are peo- ple who feared leaving this world, feared going Beyond, and as a result find themselves still in the world of the living but no longer of it. Nick can't help.

As *Harry Potter and the Deathly Hallows* begins, Harry is forced to think about death more than ever, because the adults dearest to him have died, and have died trying to save or help him: his parents, his godfather, his mentor. The quest he shares with his friends Ron and Hermione — to destroy the Horcruxes of Lord Voldemort, the objects in which he has hidden portions of his soul — gradually opens a doorway into another one which is meant just for Harry, the quest of the Deathly Hallows. The meaning of that quest is revealed to Harry, though he does not at the time understand it, in one of the most moving scenes in the whole series: his pilgrimage to Godric's Hollow, the village where he was born and where his parents died. There he finds his parents' tombstone, upon which is written an epitaph: *The last enemy that shall be destroyed is death.*

Were Voldemort to read this epitaph, he would surely be impressed, and perhaps see it as a terse and accurate summation of his life's goal. That's why Harry is shocked: his parents' tombstone reminds him of the Death Eaters. (Surely the epitaph was chosen by Dumbledore, who also chose another one in that very graveyard: it is also a verse from Scrip- ture.) Hermione tells him that the phrase means something different, but I doubt that she any more than Harry knows that it is a quotation from 1 Corinthians 15, where St. Paul explains the Resurrection of Jesus Christ.

The formal quest of the Deathly Hallows begins soon after this, and from there the story increasingly focuses on one overwhelming question: What does it mean to defeat death? Voldemort thinks he knows. The legends that have attached themselves to the Deathly Hallows — three powerful magical objects that, those legends say, give to their possessor "mastery over death" — yield an answer less wicked in its implications but no less mistaken. The proper answer to the question is found in "The Tale of the Three Brothers," and in 1 Corinthians 15, for those who have ears to hear. In the second half of this final Harry Potter story we watch our hero discern this answer, confront its implications, and discover whether he has the courage to face them. For courage is required; great courage indeed.

Many readers have already exclaimed that Harry's final quest marks him as a clear Christ figure. This is wrong, seriously wrong, and I think J. K. Rowling goes out of her way to tell us so. People (characters in the books as well as readers) think that Harry is a unique person of unique power, but at a dozen points in the series we are clearly shown that he is not: he is called the Chosen One, but he is chosen by Voldemort, and Dumbledore emphasizes to Harry the sheer contingency of this choice. The work of the Cross is done by Christ alone; Harry always has help. (It's worth emphasizing that while each of the Horcruxes is destroyed, each is destroyed by a different person.) At his moment of agony Christ was abandoned; at the end of his quest Harry is supported and comforted. As my friend Jay Wood has noted, if Harry resembles a biblical figure it is not Christ but rather Stephen the Protomartyr. But the comparisons with Stephen are limited too: for a more precise analogue, I encourage you to rummage through your children's books until you find an old copy of *The Tales of Beedle the Bard.* Surely you have one. Read the story of the Three Brothers, and pay particular attention to the youngest. You'd be surprised what you could learn.

It should be obvious at this point that the Harry Potter books amount to something more, far more, than your average penny dreadful. But they belong, firmly, to that moral universe, even as they expand it beyond what we might have thought possible. Many years ago Umberto Eco wrote that the greatness of *Casablanca* stems from its shameless deployment of every narrative cliché known to humankind: "Two clichés make us laugh. A hundred clichés move us. For we sense dimly that the clichés are *talking among themselves,* and celebrating a reunion." The Harry Potter books are like that: every trope and trick of the penny dreadful raised to the highest power and revealed in all their glory.

It seems to me especially important to keep in mind the "plainer and better gospel" of the penny dreadful when we consider the much-maligned epilogue of *Deathly Hallows*. Is it really so vital that we learn what professions the surviving characters chose to follow? If a genie allowed me to look into a portion of my own son's future for a moment, would I ask "Oh please, please tell me, what's his line of work?" Or would I prefer to know whether he marries, and whether he has children, and whether his childhood friends remain his friends always, and whether those bonds of affection continue into the next generation? The answer seems to me obvious. But perhaps that marks me as incurably bourgeois.

What do we choose to imagine, when we choose? The answer is always revelatory, which is one of the reasons Chesterton was right to say that "the simple need for some kind of ideal world in which fictitious persons play an unhampered part is infinitely deeper and older than the rules of good art, and much more important." The Harry Potter books remind us of this, and they can be, if we read them rightly, both a delight in themselves and a school for our own imaginings. They have many flaws, but I have not dwelt on them here because I forgive J. K. Rowling for every one. Her seven books are, and thank God for it, always on the side of life.

Part 2

SIGNS AND WONDERS

Reading the Signs

I WILL ALWAYS remember the day I discovered the concept of irony — not the word; that would come much later. But when I did learn the word, a smile of recognition spread across my face and an image came to my mind.

I was perhaps six or seven years old. It was a hot summer's day in Birmingham, Alabama, and I was making my more-or-less daily pilgrimage to Snappy's Service Station to get a Coke. A new Chevron emporium stood nearby, but its Cokes came only from a modern coin-operated machine. At Snappy's you had to fish them out of a big red waist-high cooler with a sliding glass door on top, and then you had to pay at the register, but it was worth it because the drinks often were slightly slushy with ice. My friends and I scorned the modern machines.

But as I approached Snappy's on my banana-seated red bike, my mood of anticipation was suddenly broken, and I braked to a quick stop. There in front of the station a car had crashed into a light post — and, to judge from the condition of the car's front end, had done so at a significant rate of speed. No one was in the car or nearby, nor, as I watched, did any ambulance or police car turn up, so perhaps the accident had happened some time earlier. The only movement at the scene came from the rectangular plate dangling by a single bolt from the front of the car, swaying a little in the hot breeze. It read GOD IS MY CO-PILOT.

Aside from the discovery of irony, I had also learned how much meaning can be crammed into just a few words, at least if the circumstances are right. And it is a belief in the power of brevity that underlies the strange activities described in two new books of photographs: *Church Signs Across America* by Steve and Pam Paulson and *Bible Road: Signs of Faith in the American Landscape* by Sam Fentress. Both books are entertaining and occasionally quite funny, but when I put them down I was surprised to discover how sad I had just become. I think there was just too much irony.

To judge by the content of these books, church signs are more likely to strive for humor than ones put up by individuals. That may have something to do with the fact that many churches come with signboards, and those boards have to be filled up — so why not fill them with something funny? Plus a church can seem a little uncared for if the sign isn't changed once in a while. So not all the signs photographically collected by the Paulsons suggest that great care was taken in their making. After you look through a few dozen of them, though, you start noticing patterns, and one of the pleasures of perusing *Church Signs Across America* is the organizational game you can end up playing. So herewith are my core principles of categorization:

Religious or Nonreligious: There are 162 photographs in the Paulsons' book, and roughly a fourth of them have no religious content whatsoever. Some defy my taxonomic skills, either because they're on the borderline (PLAN AHEAD — IT WAS NOT RAINING WHEN NOAH BUILT THE ARK has a biblical reference but no necessary spiritual meaning) or because they're incomprehensible: What does CHECK UP BEFORE YOU CHECK OUT mean? Did it get transplanted from the dentist's office? To judge from these signs, Americans have two primary shortcomings: We talk too much, and we don't smile enough. There are many variations on these themes: A CLOSED MOUTH GATHERS NO FOOT, for instance, and IF SOMEONE IS WITHOUT A SMILE, GIVE THEM YOURS.

But variety is the spice of church-sign life. We also get financial advice (A BUDGET HELPS US TO LIVE BELOW OUR YEARNINGS), assistance in child-rearing (ONE WAY TO MAKE CHILDREN MISERABLE IS TO GIVE THEM EVERYTHING THEY WANT!), and general guidance for relationships (BEST WAY TO HAVE THE LAST WORD: APOLOGIZE). As

I reflect on the wisdom dispensed in these nugget-size units, I wonder whether such signs fairly represent the teaching that goes on in their churches, or whether they are evangelistic ploys based on the principle that you begin by giving people something helpfully non-threatening and then, once you've caught their interest, hit them with the gospel. Alas, there's no way to tell. But it's interesting to note that, if the Paulsons' book is a reliable guide, you're just as likely to get a vague moral uplift from an Assembly of God or a Southern Baptist church as from a Unitarian or an Episcopal one.

Humorous or Serious: Most of the signs want to be funny, though in varying ways. The humor tends to be pretty genial, with far too much reliance on bad puns, but sarcasm and even plain bitterness make their appearances. The pastor of the Wesleyan church in Smyrna, Delaware, must have struggled through one too many stewardship campaigns by the time he made the sign reading TITHE IF YOU LOVE JESUS! ANYONE CAN HONK! I wonder what kinds of sermons you hear in the First Assembly of God of Valdosta, Georgia, which proudly bears the message ETERNITY: SMOKING OR NONSMOKING. And I have to admire the person who has simply had enough of the whole pithy-saying enterprise: SIGN BROKEN — MESSAGE INSIDE THIS SUNDAY.

Biblical or Nonbiblical: I was surprised to see that in the whole of the Paulsons' book only a half-dozen signs were composed of Bible verses — including one church in Corinth, Kentucky, which cut the Gordian knot of ever-changing signage by erecting a permanent red-brick diptych with the Ten Commandments engraved on it. (Here we stand, we can do no other.) The Paulsons do show us a few vague biblical references, like the one that reads DON'T GIVE UP! MOSES WAS ONCE A BASKET CASE! — a message that assumes a little more biblical literacy than seems to me warranted. But, in general, the sign makers shy away from the Bible. I wonder if the Paulsons' collection is representative in this respect: Did they not bother to record many biblical signs because they wished to highlight human, um, creativity?

Positive or Negative: Perhaps some subdividing is called for here, since the positive messages can be words of encouragement, reassurance, or exhortation, while the negative ones can take the form of warning or blunt threat. Though, again, there is the occasional sarcasm

(WHAT PART OF "THOU SHALT NOT" DON'T YOU UNDERSTAND?), the negativity tends to be pretty earnest and preoccupied with the likelihood of the Second Coming; the encouragement and exhortation are likewise earnest but in a more lighthearted you-can-*do*-it kind of way.

Reading through *Church Signs Across America,* I found myself asking which of these churches I would attend if I had to decide on the basis of the signs alone — omitting, since I am a Protestant, the Catholic ones, though not without regret, since the only sayings of great Christians in the whole book are found on Catholic churches' signs. (I must say that LORD, MAKE ME AN INSTRUMENT OF YOUR PEACE and OUR HEARTS ARE RESTLESS UNTIL THEY FIND THEIR REST IN YOU look a little funny in all caps.) In general I was more attracted to the negative ones. Their pugnaciousness suggests a certain indifference to public opinion that is, or at least can be, commendable in a Christian community. Plus, I know that I would never, ever attend a church that had used its sign space to encourage me to smile more often. But, despite my Eeyorish inclination, I could not suppress a grin at one of the saccharine ones: IF GOD HAD A REFRIGERATOR, YOUR PICTURE WOULD BE ON IT.

If the church signs can seem perfunctory at times, the religious signs in barbershop windows — or on the blank brick walls of garages, barns, or even private houses — don't need to be there. No one would miss them if they were absent, which yields them a fierce immediacy. The people who create them are probably a little too intense for humor: You hope not to end up waiting in line with one of them at the DMV, and you don't want one to take the stool next to yours at the local diner.

This urgency gives a tense energy to all these signs, even the seemingly casual and funny ones. It's nearly palpable, the sign makers' fear that we will pass by, at speed, focused on other things — worldly things that keep God far from our minds — and their conviction that only something exceptionally vivid has a chance of catching our attention. It's the visual equivalent of shouting. Flannery O'Connor once defended her own methods of fiction writing by saying that "to the hard of hearing you shout, and for the almost blind you draw large startling figures." These signs are like that, and, indeed, the title of one of O'Connor's most famous stories, "The Life You Save May Be Your Own," is borrowed from a billboard encouraging people to drive safely.

The photographs by Sam Fentress powerfully capture this intensity. *Bible Road* is a very different book from *Church Signs Across America,* in large part because the Paulsons stood in front of a lot of signs and took snapshots of them, whereas Fentress is a gifted artist whose photographs embrace the varying moods and textures of the many distinctly American scenes he portrays. (Several of these photographs first appeared in the October 2001 issue of *FIRST THINGS.*)

JESUS THE LIGHT OF THE WORLD reads one of the messages Fentress captures. In fluorescent lighting exactly like that on a cheap motel — there's even a slightly tilted bright yellow star in one corner — the image is set in the evening sky, wrapped in the deep purple of the last moments of dusk. (The light shone in the darkness, and the darkness comprehended it not.) Fentress's pictures are often in just this way sympathetic with their subjects: They cooperate with and even accentuate the mood of the signs themselves. When the message is blunt and stark, so too is the photograph. Here's what Fentress saw in Jackson, Mississippi, in 1985, on a rented lit-from-within sign with black letters stuck on:

JESUS SAID YE MUST BE

BORN AGAIN JOHN 3-7

AREA SIZE RUG SALE

20% OFF

A simple straightforward message from a simple straightforward world. Fentress shot it with black-and-white film and allowed the sign to fill nearly the whole frame.

In contrast to the Paulsons' church signs, Fentress's images — on buses, on the signs of interstate-exit truck stops, on telephone poles, on flat rocks, on almost anything — are overwhelmingly biblical, as his title suggests. Even where they are not direct quotations, they refer to biblical events or teachings, or they name the names of God, or — as on a carefully but amateurishly hand-painted message planted on a roadside in Prattville, Alabama — they just say READ THE BIBLE.

The simplicity intensifies the urgency: Sometimes you get the sense that people could write only a few words, or even one word, before being taken hostage by criminals, or dying of some strange blood disease, or suffering abduction by aliens. Someone has spray-painted on a stainless-steel electrical box, "God says, Faith Without Work Dead" — this distinctive medium allows the use of non-capital letters, though it would have been nice if the painter had been attentive to certain other matters, like the distinction between "work" and "works." Elsewhere we see a flat stone outcrop on an Alaskan roadside bearing in white paint or chalk the single name JESUS. On the facing page there's another slab of rock, this one somewhere in Harlem, with shakier and much smaller lettering: OBEY GOD OR BURN it reads, and the writer, with the precision of the insane, has ended the sentence with a neat white period.

Signs like this are created and then left to find such audiences as they may. They are not meant to be revised or erased. Others are scarcely less permanent: An old barn covered with fading Bible verses *could* be painted over and remessaged, but that's not likely. Looking at the signs that Fentress captures, one gets the sense that their makers decided to say the single most important thing they could think of and leave it at that. A notable exception to this rule is a house in Winchester, Missouri, that Fentress photographed four times in 1987 and 1988. Though the scene hardly varies — it's one end of the aluminum-sided house, with two rectangular windows over two garage doors — signs of changing seasons are visible: A barbecue grill appears in one photo; a big stack of firewood in another.

And in each photograph there's a different message, displayed in foot-high black letters affixed to the siding: IF SINGLE, DON'T ACT LIKE YOU'RE MARRIED. IF MARRIED, DON'T ACT LIKE YOU'RE SINGLE; then IF YOU'RE NOT TOTALLY SAVED, YOU ARE TOTALLY LOST. READ JOHN CHAPTER 3; then ALCOHOL, DRUGS, SEX AND SUICIDE ONLY ADD TO YOUR TROUBLES. JESUS IS THE ONLY ANSWER; and finally LORD, GIVE ME COURAGE TO PART WITH WHAT I HOLD DEAR, IF IT SEPARATES ME FROM YOU.

I stared at the page with these four messages for a long time before I realized that someone had turned the side of his house into a vast analogue to a blog. Like a blog, this house records a person's thoughts, whether those thoughts are directed toward the author or toward the audience; as on a blog, the recorded thoughts are available for anyone to read who happens to pass by. One difference between this inscribed house and the average blog is that the house inscriber knows that "you're" has an apostrophe and can spell "separates." But an even bigger difference is that a blog retains all its previous posts, while this technology demands that each new entry eliminate its predecessors. Sam Fentress's photos help remedy that deficiency, but one does not learn from Fentress how often the message was changed. Maybe these four messages are but a tiny selection; maybe the message was renewed daily and over the course of weeks or months covered all the categories I listed earlier in my inventory of church signs: exhortation, reassurance, warning, threat. . . . I wouldn't expect many laughs, though.

Thinking about what I have called the urgency of these messages — even the ridiculous jokes on the church signs suggest a clown's insistence, a look-at-me pleading — I am inclined to reconsider something I said at the outset of this essay. Maybe it's not "a belief in the power of brevity" prompting these signs. Maybe it's a panicky recognition that sometimes brevity is all you get: *Tell us the meaning of life in no more than ten words.* If brevity is the soul of wit, perhaps desperation is the soul of brevity.

The people who write apocalyptic or consoling or hortatory messages on their houses and barns, or nail them to their fence posts, might well tell you stories, long stories if they had any opportunity at all to do so. They would weave for you tales of God's wrath or love, and of how their lives were transformed by the very knowledge that they now are pleased to share with you.

But they never get that chance. So they shout at us and draw large startling figures for us as we speed by. The writers stay put, or at least their signs do, while we zoom through town, nearly unrecognizable blurs who may not have sense enough to ask the only question that really matters: What must I do to be saved?

The Secret Garden

LOOKING THROUGH the many and lavish illustrations of Alessandro Scafi's *Mapping Paradise: A History of Heaven on Earth,* I find myself drawn again and again to a photograph reproduced near the book's end. It appeared originally in the *Times* of London and was taken in 1944 in the town of Qurna in Iraq, near the confluence of the Tigris and Euphrates rivers. One of those rivers fills the picture's background, and in the foreground is an octagonal wall of pale brick, perhaps three feet high, like a baptismal font. Within the wall is a dead tree, which seems to have fallen so that two bare branches sink into the dirt outside the font.

The branches angle strangely, giving the vivid appearance of an enormous insect, a praying mantis crawling out of the font and onto the surrounding bare dirt, there no doubt to perish. A carefully made sign at the top of the wall, canted awkwardly against the tree's dead trunk, reads: "The Original GARDEN of EDEN." Locals call the tree the Tree of Adam, that is, the Tree of Knowledge of Good and Evil. Though living branches with leaves may be seen in the background of the photograph, my research suggests that it is not the Tree of Life. It's just a tree.

Perhaps not too long after that photograph was taken, the people of Qurna planted a replacement for the Tree of Adam, but it died too: Its straighter but equally bare trunk stands there today. The ironies of the scene are journalistic and irresistible, which is why the *Times* sent people there in 1944, in time of war, and again in 2003, also in time of war, to meditate upon contemporary tragedies. The problem with Paradise is that it's always Lost, of course; any meditation on it, especially in a place that claims to be its geographical location, is bound to be ironic or elegaic or both.

And yet, as Scafi's remarkable *Mapping Paradise* demonstrates, there have been centuries of attempts to place paradise on maps, thereby making it somehow present to our world or at least possibly present. Paradise is always lost, but maps are for finding.

Now, finding isn't everything: In the *Inferno*, Dante the pilgrim meets the shade of Ulysses, whose wanderlust led him to explore what Dante the poet believed to be the "Hemisphere of Water," that half of the earth covered by the seas except for a single mountainous island in the midst of it called the Mount of Purgatory. (Start digging straight down at Mount Calvary and eventually you'll make your way to it, though only by passing through Hell.) At the top of this mountain sits the earthly paradise, which those who have been fully cleansed of sin are allowed to enter: They have become like Adam before the Fall. But Ulysses sees none of this. As soon as he gets within sight of the mountain, God sends a great storm to sweep his ship under the waves.

Still, if finding isn't everything, at least it's something. To see — delineated on a sheet that includes or could include Athens, Greece, and Athens, Georgia — the place where God first shaped man from the dust! Canterbury Cathedral in England once possessed, and for all I know still possesses, a little of the clay from which God made Adam (presumably the leftovers and trimmings), and, if this alone was sufficient to enchant pilgrims, still greater would be the awe experienced from merely picturing the spot where the Divine Hand reached down and scooped up the earth. To think that the tree in which the serpent entwined himself and from which Eve plucked the fruit once stood, and maybe even still stands, on the same ground that we walk! The theme of Scafi's book is the power of this idea: that paradise belongs to the world that we recognize as our own, that perfection was found in the same continuum of space that we know in all its brokenness. To map paradise is to feel grief for what has been lost and hope for what may be restored. Scafi's exploration of this history can be pedantic at times — the opening chapter, alas, is a history of histories of the mapping of paradise — but his research is impeccable and the illustrations are astounding. Especially welcome are the many redrawings of medieval maps, by Scafi himself, that make their outlines clearer and translate their often-obscure labels into clear English. And there is a powerful story here: how through the history of Christianity confidence in the human ability to map Eden — and in the very legitimacy and validity of the project — waxed and then waned.

A point of great controversy in the early Church concerned whether Eden was indeed a geographically specific place on this globe. For some theologians — most notably Origen of Alexandria, who had inherited this line of thought from the first-century Jewish thinker Philo — a physical paradise was almost unthinkable, unworthy of God. The topic prompted one of the classic battles between the Alexandrian school of exegesis, which consistently read the Genesis narrative allegorically, and the school of Antioch, which read it historically and literally. From the Antiochan tradition, John Chrysostom and Theodore of Mopsuestia condemn the allegorical reading as fiercely as Origen had denounced the literal.

It remained for Augustine effectively to resolve the debate by saying, with perhaps uncharacteristic irenicism, that both sides were right: The story of Adam and Eve in the Garden does indeed describe a historical event but one that God has shaped so that it was full of allegorical and typological significance. This would become the normal, if not unanimously held, position of Christians for many centuries, but it raised an interesting series of questions in its turn: Where, then, was this physical paradise? Might it still be in its original location? If so, could it be found? If it were found, would angels with flaming swords still be guarding its gates?

The first geographical hint offered by the narrative arrives at Genesis 2:8: "And the Lord God planted a garden in Eden, in the east, and there he put the man whom he had formed." For titans of the Church like Isidore of Seville and the Venerable Bede (a century later), this could only mean that Eden was set in the uttermost East of the world. The easternmost land Bede had heard of — from his reading of Pliny the Elder's *Natural History* — was India, so he suspected that Eden could be found there, or nearby.

So when the *mappae mundi* — maps of the whole world — began to be made in the Middle Ages, paradise was placed in the extreme East, often near that many-named island then known as Taprobana, later as Serendip and Ceylon and Sri Lanka. (Thus the seventh-century scholar Isidore of Seville would write, in what sounds to us like a deadpan comic tone: "Asia includes many provinces and regions. I shall briefly list their names and locations, starting with Paradise.") Anyone accustomed to reading modern maps will be puzzled by these medieval representations of our world, for shapes and distances often seem crazily distorted. But, as Scafi wisely points out, "The first thing to bear in mind when looking at paradise on a medieval *mappa mundi* is that this kind of map was not created to inform the observer of the precise latitude, longitude, and size of the Garden of Eden, but to demonstrate its contiguity to the inhabited earth." Scafi calls this "topological mapping," and it scarcely disappeared with the end of the Middle Ages. The famous multicolored map of the London Underground is topological, caring nothing for relative distances or even for strict orientation (its lines move only vertically, horizontally, and at 45-degree angles). Previous depictions of the Underground had been confusing to the point of uselessness because they included precise information about distances and directions that are frankly irrelevant to people riding on trains, which, after all, are underground. Fair to say that riders need to know only (a) whether they are on the proper line, (b) whether they are headed in the proper direction, and (c) how many stops away their destination is.

So the point of placing the earthly paradise on a *mappa mundi* is not to show people how to get there but to make the theological point that Eden really was here, in our world — indeed was the heart of our world, was what our world was supposed to be and would still be had Adam not disobeyed God. "The two key criteria in the mapping of paradise," writes Scafi, are "that it must be shown as adjacent to, but not part of, the inhabited earth and that it should be prominent." It occupies the same spatial continuum that we do, but must be marked as somehow separate in order to reinforce the message of the Fall. Thus some maps place it across a great sea, others across a vast desert or wilderness, others atop a great mountain. (Bede thought it had to be atop the highest mountain so it could escape the flood that submerged the rest of the world, a thought that perhaps also governs Dante's placement of it.)

One of the most striking and powerful elements of Scafi's book is his insistence that such geographical conceptions marry a biblical picture of space and a biblical account of time. Beatus of Liébana's commentary on the Book of Revelation, contemporaneous with the great Vatican map, includes its own map of the world in order to show where and how the gospel has spread throughout the world. His map is therefore, to some degree, a map of salvation history. When, some centuries later, Hugh of St. Victor speaks of the world in its spatial aspect, he uses the term *mundus;* when he speaks of it in its temporal aspect, he uses the term *saeculum.* Medieval mapping is a way of connecting the *mundus* to the *saeculum.* So one of the reasons these maps are often oriented to the East — and of course orient means "east" — is that this puts the earthly paradise at the top or beginning of the map and thereby at least gestures toward a historical dimension. Among the most famous of all the *mappae mundi,* the great and astonishingly detailed Hereford Map at England's Hereford Cathedral reinforces this point, not only by placing the earthly paradise at the top of the map, but also by adding, as a kind of crown to the circle of the world, a portrayal of Christ's Second Coming in Judgment, with images on either side of him of people going to blessedness or to damnation. The physical proximity of this image of Christ to the circular walled garden of paradise — which is just below his feet — reminds us of what he comes again to restore.

Perhaps even more striking is the still vaster Ebstorf world map, which portrays a world that obscures Christ and yet is embraced by him: His head is visible at the top, a hand emerges at the North and South, and the feet poke out below the Pillars of Hercules. As Scafi points out, one way to look at this map is to see the world as "a gigantic eucharistic Host." (The map was destroyed in an Allied bombing raid on the German city of Hanover in 1943.) Likewise, regions on these maps are often divided according to biblical events or histories. For instance, a map now in Lambeth Palace shows how the whole world was divided among the sons of Noah; and the aforementioned map of

94

Beatus of Liébana divides the world among the twelve apostles according to their geographical responsibilities for preaching the gospel.

This imaging of the world as a *mundus* and *saeculum* established by apostolic mission finds a powerful modern proponent in the great and strange Eugen Rosenstock-Huessy, a German-Jewish convert to Catholicism who came to the United States when the Nazis took power, taught at Harvard and then Dartmouth, and wrote an enormous book called *Out of Revolution: Autobiography of Western Man* (1938) that won great admiration from W. H. Auden and Reinhold Niebuhr. The book is, in effect, nothing more than a vast and detailed interpretation of the last thousand years of Western history as an elaboration of Beatus's great map of apostolic proclamation.

Scafi makes the interesting point that many world travelers from the High Middle Ages onward — Marco Polo and his ilk — are fascinated by the legend of Prester John's kingdom and other such fabulous tales of exotic kingdoms and strange places, yet they never talk about paradise. It's just not on their itinerary. In the early medieval period, there had, of course, been the many legends surrounding Saint Brendan, but in his journeys a quest for the Garden of Eden becomes mixed and confused with the quest for the *terra repromissionis sanctorum,* the "Land of the Promise of the Saints," a kind of Christianized version of the ancient writers' Elysian Fields. In some medieval legends, Alexander the Great is a seeker after Eden, as is Ulysses in Dante, but once Europeans start traveling well beyond Europe they show little inclination to imitate these great heroes of history and legend. The semi-fictitious traveler John Mendeville mentions Eden but only to say that he doesn't consider himself worthy of going there. Somewhat later, Christopher Columbus would affirm his belief in the continuing geographical reality of the earthly paradise but insists that no one could ever travel to it.

Perhaps this is just as well, because what C. S. Lewis might call the Medieval Model of Eden's place on earth was never without strenuous controversy, and eventually there arose people like the philosopher Duns Scotus who were prepared to demolish all the existing theories. Eden is in the far East? Well, the notion of "East" is a relative one, Scotus said: Wherever you are, you're always east of something and west of something else. Paradise is situated at the equator? Nah, too hot for what must, in the biblical account, be a perfectly temperate garden. As for Bede's atop-the-highest-mountain theory, the air in such a location would be far too thin. It appears that Scotus did believe in a physical paradise, but he did not think it was accessible to the developing tools of natural philosophy, or what we would call experimental science. But, in that case, what becomes of the idea that paradise is part of the world we now live in? What becomes of the idea that it belongs on our maps? "From about 1500 onwards," Scafi writes, "no map of the world showed the earthly paradise."

Scafi explains that the great age of nautical exploration that accompanies, and hastens, the advent of the Renaissance had a profound effect on the practice of cartography in Europe. After all, when errors in navigation can run your ship onto rocks, drowning your cargo and perhaps your crew as well, topological maps that ignore proportional size and relative distance are worse than useless; they are potentially deadly. But perhaps even more disruptive than the rise of the nautical chart was the discovery of one of the great masterpieces of Western learning, Ptolemy's *Geography,* written in the second century A.D., with its atlas of twenty-seven maps of various parts of the world. A Byzantine manuscript of this book arrived in Venice in 1406 and was soon thereafter copied and distributed all over Europe. Oddly, Ptolemy's geography began to exert a kind of dominance at almost the same time that, thanks to Copernicus and others, his cosmology began to decline in influence.

One aspect of Ptolemy's maps would prove to be especially revolutionary: They were all oriented to the North. Once Western European cartographers began imitating this practice, then paradise was displaced from its "narrative" position at the top of a map and the bond between *mundus* and *saeculum* was broken. As soon as maps are oriented to the North (or indeed anywhere but the East), the earthly paradise starts to disappear from them, because under the Ptolemaic influence maps become purely spatial rather than continuing their earlier spatio-temporal character. Maps of the world were severed from the biblical narrative, and indeed Scafi's book causes me to wonder if what Hans Frei famously called "the eclipse of biblical narrative" is not significantly related to the history of cartography, something that Frei and other tellers of this tale have scarcely considered. What Weber called the "disenchantment of the world" may have gotten a head start when mapmakers displaced Eden from its traditional place of primacy.

Scafi asserts that the first scholar — by whom he must mean the first orthodox scholar — to claim that the earthly paradise no longer exists at all was one Augustine Steuchus, a bishop who in 1542 became prefect of the Vatican Library. On the basis of the kind of textual and historical scholarship we usually associate with early Protestantism, Steuchus argued that Scripture clearly indicates Eden was located not in the far East — the "Eden, in the east" line from Genesis 2:8 had been for all those centuries a lamentable red herring — but rather, and quite obviously, in Mesopotamia.

Moreover, he continued, Eden could not have been separated in any significant way from the rest of the world, else what would have been the point of posting angelic guards around it? And anyone who wished to see it would have been motivated by curiosity rather than greed, for after the Fall the perfect Garden became just another wild and unculti-vated spot of land, distinguished only by those mighty guardians. Then the Flood, which according to the text was clearly universal, utterly de-stroyed the spot, which relieved the angels of what had surely been a tedious duty and made any discovery of Eden forever impossible.

The idea that the Flood had wiped out all evidence of the earthly paradise's location had already been articulated by Martin Luther. Steuchus and Luther also agreed that the traditional interpretations of the four rivers mentioned in Genesis 2:10-14 — some earlier maps had shown them flowing into the ground in a far-eastern Eden and then emerging again in Mesopotamia — were wildly misbegotten, and that one could reasonably conclude the Garden of Eden had been located somewhere between the Tigris and the Euphrates. The point of their confluence is rather farther south than Steuchus thought the Garden was likely to have been, but he was willing to consider that spot as a possibility. John Calvin, by contrast, did not think the deluge had been quite so devastating; indeed, he believed that the same four rivers that flow through Mesopotamia today were the ones that flowed through that land in Edenic times, and that this continuity is a sign of God's con-tinuing benevolence to us.

In reading the later chapters of Scafi's book, I found it curious that this one issue — the location of the four rivers and their correspondence, or lack of correspondence, to present-day streams — would come to dominate debate about the location of Eden almost to the exclusion of other matters. From Sir Walter Raleigh's map in his *History of the World* (1617), to Pierre-Daniel Huet's *Traité de la situation du paradis terrestre* (1691), to Paul Wright's *New Map of the Garden and the Land of Eden* (1782), all the way to Albert R. Terry's *The Flood and Garden of Eden: Astounding Facts and Prophecies* (1962), it's all about the rivers. The later history of mapping paradise is continually beset by confusion and frustration on this point: attempts to figure out, first, what the Bible actually says about them and, second, how that might be reconciled with growing knowledge of the actual geography of the region are endlessly disputed. ("A river flowed out of Eden to water the garden, and there it divided and became four rivers," says Genesis, and it names two of those rivers as the Tigris and the Euphrates, which quite obviously do not have a single source.) Scafi is perhaps too detailed in his coverage of his subject, but there's no doubt that the rivers became a topic of hot controversy precisely because they raised in unique ways the increasingly dominant problem in the Western world of how to reconcile biblical testimony with scientific discovery, especially as in the nineteenth century the new science of archaeology rises and develops. Archaeology has, overall, done far more to reinforce and support the biblical narrative than most practitioners in the field ever imagined it could, but it has left the quest for a geographically definite Eden in permanent and irrecoverable disarray. There are, of course, still a handful of cranks and oddballs searching for Eden or believing that they have discovered it through some combination of geography, textual criticism, trigonometry, and personal revelation. But more common is the attitude taken by the makers of the "Map to Heaven and the City of Life," produced a few years ago by Champion Gospel Publications of Daytona Beach, Florida.

Here the King's Highway emerges from "THE WORLD," skirts the Lake of Fire, and heads upward (on the old *mappae mundi,* that would have meant eastward, but we are beyond geography here) toward Heaven through the various suburbs of the Godly life: the dense networks of streets in Truth and Church; the prosperous riverside communities of Baptism and Discipleship; and there, on the far bank of Righteousness River, the culs-de-sac of Love, with its forested parkland, and the oddly underdeveloped and sparsely populated Giving. We get to this highway from our well-appointed homes on Covenant Street or Reconciliation Way or (perhaps my favorite) Unspeakable Drive. But, by the grace of God, we make it to the Highway and follow it until it passes into Rapture Field and becomes Resurrection Runway and shoots us into the clouds to meet the Lord.

Perhaps you feel your view of paradise is unlike this one? Nevertheless, in the long story of these maps and of an imaginative world progressively disenchanted and disoriented, we're all allegorists now, all members of the Alexandrian school, though Origen might blanch to see the company he's now keeping. Meanwhile, far away in Qurna, perhaps by now they have planted another Tree of Adam.

The Life of Trees

I HAVE COME late to the knowledge of trees, and while I would like to think that I have loved them all my life, that's probably not really true. Had I loved them all along I would know more about them by now. The most enlightening and attractive writers about trees seem to have been lifelong aficionados — one book I recently read begins, "Having been partly arboreal since the age of eight, I . . ." — and the ease with which they describe their old friends shames me a bit. Reading them, I feel much the same envy I feel when watching an experienced skater flow across an iced-over pond.

In the preface to his first collection of essays, *Happy to Be Here,* Garrison Keillor explains how he came to realize that the years he spent, at the outset of his career, trying to write a big novel were just wasted. Looking back on that fruitless time, when piles of typed pages grew on his desk without amounting to anything more than piles of typed pages, he came to see that his ignorance of trees was emblematic of his difficulties. The novel-in-progress itself

> lay on a shelf over the radiator, and next to it stood the typewriter stand, up against a window that looked out on an elm tree and a yellow bungalow with blue trim, across the street. I assume it was an elm because it died that spring during an elm epidemic and the city foresters cut it down, but in fact there are only four or five plants I can identify with certainty and the elm is not one of them. I

regret this but there it is: plant life has never been more to me than a sort of canvas backdrop. There was a houseplant in that bedroom too, some type of vine or vine-related plant, and it also died.

The characters in his novel, he says, spent a lot of time smoking while propped against trees; but what kind of trees he did not say. Nor did he care. In retrospect Keillor saw that the story grew dull and lifeless because its fictional world was so skimpily furnished; characters who devoted so much time to "leaning against vague vegetation" could scarcely expect to be worthy of a reader's time.

I have spent much of my own life surrounded by vegetation equally vague, though I rarely lean on any of it and haven't smoked since I was about sixteen. For one thing, as a child I was anything but arboreal: my fear of heights confined my tree-climbing to the apple and peach trees in my neighbor's garden, where I could barely get six feet off the ground, and while I could identify those trees when fruit was hanging from them, in other seasons I would have been out of luck. Almost the only tree I could name with confidence was the pecan, because our yard was full of mature, heavily-bearing pecan trees that dumped thousands of nuts on the ground every fall. (I was distinctly shocked when we moved from that house and I discovered that people paid large sums of money for pecans. I thought of them primarily as a nuisance: one of my jobs every fall was to gather up paper grocery bags full of nuts and deliver them to the neighbors, since otherwise crossing our lawn would have been like walking on ball bearings. I figured that the neighbors were doing us a favor by taking the things off our hands.) And I am not sure that I could have identified a pecan tree if I came upon it in the springtime and if it were surrounded by other kinds of tree, or tree-related plants.

Yet the very form of Tree was endlessly fascinating to me. We lived in an old ramshackle house which had the single virtue of a large L-shaped porch, and in the frequent afternoon thunderstorms of my Alabama childhood I would park myself in a dry spot on the porch and watch, almost literally mesmerized, the tall trees' dialogue with the wind. I never tired of this spectacle, nor did I ever miss an opportunity to encounter it again. The enormous creatures really did seem almost to talk to one another, and perhaps to me. Just a few weeks ago, when powerful southerly winds rushed into my part of Illinois, I was walking across the wide front lawn of the Wheaton College campus, and when I passed under an enormous oak I heard that same language and felt transported to that porch in Alabama and our cluster of pecan trees. But I didn't pause in reverie; instead I quickened my pace, because in winds so fierce that old oak could easily have dropped a branch big enough to kill me.

That trees strike us as human-like is an essential element of their fascination but is also part of the fear they can inspire. Their proportions resemble ours; their crowns are like heads, their branches arms — no wonder so many of the myths Ovid records in the *Metamorphoses* have people turned into them. They are the visually dominant figures of the plant kingdom, as we fancy ourselves the monarchs of the animal realm. Like us, they can in their solitude seem welcoming and friendly, though sometimes imposing; also like us, in mass they can terrify. Who has understood better than Tolkien the terrors and the companionable appeal of trees, and the way those traits are mixed imperceptibly together? In Fangorn Forest we see the first tempered by the second; in Treebeard and the other Ents the second tempered by the first. Yet in depicting these creatures of the woods Tolkien seems to many of us to have created nothing, but rather to have read our minds, and sometimes our nightmares.

On the east side of the house I now live in we have a little sunporch or Florida room where I camp out whenever the weather allows it. From my usual seat I look out across our back yard, which is open and flat but bordered by trees. An enormous twin-trunked honey locust dominates the far side of the lawn; in the back is a tall Norway spruce and a small redbud which seems to be thriving since the recent death of a crabapple that had partially blocked its sunshine. Nearest to me, and most often in my sight and mind, is a maple — but what kind of maple? The shape of the leaves is unmistakable, so that determines the species; and everything about the tree, from the texture of the bark, to its delightful helicopterish "keys" with their cargo of seed, to its droopy smaller branches and its tendency to drop lots of twigs, fairly shouts that it's a silver maple. Except for one thing: the undersides of the leaves, the very feature that gives the silver maple its name, aren't silver at all. I sometimes tell myself that they're grayish-green, but really they aren't: they're just a pale green with a matte surface. There are other silver maples in my neighborhood that anyone could recognize immediately by those highly distinctive leaves.

Individual trees within a species, and even within a distinct variety, can vary tremendously (just think about the many sizes, shapes, and colors of people), so it's perfectly possible that this lack of silveriness is well within the bounds of ordinary variation; but nevertheless it remains a source of annoyance to me that I can't confidently name this most familiar tree. It is very familiar to me, and beautiful. I have simply stared at it for many hours when I was supposed to be grading papers or writing essays, and even when I have set myself the task of figuring out what kind of maple it is. Its architecture endlessly delights my eye. About twelve feet off the ground its trunk divides into three distinct sub-trunks, and from them stem, at pleasing intervals that are only slightly irregular, thick branches that extend horizontally for unusually long distances. The effect is one of elegant complexity, and different aspects of this architecture attract my attention at different seasons, in the dead of winter almost as much as in the season of full leaf or in the time when the keys spin comically through the air and crash-land on my lawn and driveway.

It's when I'm in one of my tree-reveries that I best understand what the poet Gerard Manley Hopkins had in mind when he coined the terms "instress" and "inscape." By "inscape" Hopkins meant something like the unique form or structure of a particular thing; by "instress" something like an energy or resonance — a divine energy — which binds the object to its perceiver. A thing's inscape is always there; instress is discernible only by certain people at certain times. To see it is a kind of gift of the Holy Spirit. Hopkins uses these terms to describe trees more than any other thing: "There is one notable dead tree . . . the inscape markedly holding its most simple and beautiful oneness up from the ground through a graceful swerve below (I think) the spring of the branches up to the tops of the timber. I saw the inscape freshly, as if my mind were still growing, though with a companion the eye and the ear are for the most part shut and instress cannot come." I feel much the same way about my tree, my silver maple — if that's what it is.

British folk write well about trees, I find, and I have a theory to explain this, one which, like most of my theories, is virtually unencumbered by evidence. Britons aren't alone in this fascination, but it takes different forms elsewhere. Americans, for instance, tend to be fascinated by notable individual trees — the Oldest Tree in the World (a bristlecone pine), the Most Massive Tree in the World (a giant sequoia), the Tallest Tree in the World (a coast redwood), all of which are in California — while Germans love and tend to mythologize whole forests. A German might have come up with Fangorn Forest, but not Treebeard; an American, vice versa. The British, however, maintain the proper balance. I think this is because they live on an island which was once heavily forested, and retains many ancient and beautiful trees, but which people over the centuries have transformed into field and pasture and meadow. Looking at the forbidding moors of Scotland one can scarcely believe that most of that country was once densely forested; yet it is so. And the trees are missing simply because humans cut them down. So some Scots are taking pains to restore at least some of the ancient Caledonian pines; and old trees there are revered, none more so than a yew tree in Fortingall under which, it is said, Pontius Pilate once sat and thought. Similar stories can be told about Ireland and England, too.

Two recent books uphold, and extend, this great tradition: *The Tree,* by Colin Tudge, and *Woodlands,* by Oliver Rackham. Tudge is one of the best science writers I have come across — his *The Engineer in the Garden* remains, a decade after its publication, an exceptionally valuable book about biotechnology and genetic manipulation — while Rackham, a fellow of Corpus Christi College, Cambridge, is a near-legendary botanist and historical ecologist. Both men write vividly and charmingly, largely because they take such pleasure in their subjects. *Woodlands* would seem to have a more limited range than *The Tree:* after all, one of the four major sections of Tudge's book is called "All the Trees in the World," and you can't get much more ambitious than that, while Rackham's task is to describe not trees in general, but the various ways in which trees are found in groups and in relation to other creatures, particularly in Britain. (The book appears in the U.K. as a Collins New Naturalist field guide, and its historical sections in particular treat the British context exclusively.) But scattered throughout the 600 pages of

Woodlands is an education in the biology of trees about as thorough as what Tudge offers, though in a less methodical form. There is more history in Rackham, who, because of his narrower geographical compass, can show how the woodlands of Britain have waxed and waned over the centuries, either because of changing human practices or because of their relations with other creatures. Both books are delightful, and I am very glad that I read both, but if I had to recommend just one, it would have to be Tudge. Rackham only makes it to his second chapter before introducing, with evident enthusiasm, a multi-page chart accounting for "Associations between mycorrhizal agarics and trees." Tudge does not do this kind of thing at all. Thus my choice.

It is almost impossible to describe these books without falling into a recitation of Fun Facts to Know and Tell. Some trees (mangroves and their relatives) can live with their roots in ocean water because they have developed bark that filters out the salt. Coast redwoods get about a third of their water from the fogs that roll in off the Pacific — good thing, because it is no easy trick to lift water three hundred and fifty feet in the air, which is what some of these titans do. Many botanists understand a grove of aspens as one enormous organism, among the largest found in nature, though not as large as the vast fungi that can run for dozens of acres underground, providing minerals to thousands of trees. A tree endemic to the island of New Caledonia (*Sebertia acuminata,* if you must know) absorbs so much nickel that its rubbery sap runs bright blue. Many trees survive and even thrive after having been blown over in storms: they just need to keep a small portion of their root system in place. And cows — this is a typical Rackham comment — cows prefer tree leaves to almost any other food, but just can't reach many of them. Sad, really.

But perhaps the most interesting fact to be gleaned from these books — and from Richard Preston's *The Wild Trees* — is this: much of our knowledge about trees is of recent vintage, and there is still a great deal about these creatures that we do not know. Rackham points out that two great storms that swept across Britain in 1987 and 1990 and uprooted thousands of old trees created surprise and consternation in many botanists: all along they had been describing the long taproots that anchored such trees deep in the ground, but the storms revealed that the taproots didn't exist. Even the largest trees can have roots just a couple of feet deep: they extend horizontally vast distances, but the taproots that saplings (especially oaks) send down are soon supplanted. Preston describes the work of Steve Sillett, of Humboldt State University in California, and a small group of other scientists who in the past fifteen years have discovered what really goes on in the canopies of our tallest trees — something which earlier botanists had tried, with limited success, to explore by floating above the forests in balloons. Sillett and company simply climb the trees, risking life and limb every time they do it, and in the process are discovering the phenomenally complex ecosystem flourishing in those heights. Preston, who became a climber himself and joined Sillett on some of his expeditions, found in the crowns of some Eastern trees flying squirrels so unfamiliar with human beings that they allowed him to scratch their heads, and life two hundred feet farther up, in those California redwoods, is even stranger. As one scientist vividly remarked, atop some of the tallest redwoods, with their dense and interlocking multiple crowns, you could put showshoes on and throw a Frisbee around. O brave new world indeed.

I have been able to give the merest glimpse here of how fascinating trees are in themselves — even the most cursory description of their ingenious methods of feeding and growing themselves is beyond this essay's scope — but equally fascinating, perhaps, is the story of their role in human culture. This essay appears in a magazine made of paper; I wrote much of it sitting at a wooden desk, from which I arose occasionally to get an apple — an apple I bought at the local grocery after driving there in a rubber-tired vehicle. On such jaunts I may have occasionally worn a rayon shirt (rayon is made from cellulose), and I might also have picked up a bottle of olive oil, or some cinnamon sticks, or bay leaves, or a few avocados for my justly famed guacamole.

One could be forgiven for thinking that trees are co-extensive with culture itself. In his two-volume historical masterwork *The Mediterranean and the Mediterranean World in the Age of Philip II,* Fernand Braudel identifies "the Mediterranean world" with the domain of the olive tree, and any reader of the Bible or of Homer will know why he says so. One of the most powerful images in literature comes near the end of the *Odyssey,* when Odysseus describes the marriage-bed he and

Penelope shared, a bed carved from the trunk of a living olive tree. For Homer this could have been nothing less than an image of the human world, emerging from and revering the natural world as it is exemplified in the tree from which Homer's people and their descendants took the most: fruit to eat, wood for fire or furniture, oil for cooking and light and the anointing of faces.

Yet, as the aforementioned denuding of Britain suggests, humans have not always appreciated trees or our debts to them. For those who make their living from herding animals, every tree represents so many fewer square feet of pasturage; it is an impediment to life itself, or can seem so. (Often erroneously, of course.) In heavily forested areas, trees must often be banished to the periphery of human settlement in order to make that settlement possible — and to open it to sunshine that is especially welcome in cooler climates. For these reasons and others, Henry W. Lawrence explains in his *City Trees,* it was not until the 18th century that trees became a common and expected feature of European urban landscapes. Treeless urbanity seems horrible to us — the elimination of greenery is a key feature of almost all our dystopian images — but it must be remembered that in the Middle Ages cities were very small places indeed. Paris was probably the largest European city of that period, and you could walk from any one of its walled boundaries to any other in half an hour. So, though there was an absolute divide between the treeless city and the forested countryside, marked by any given city's walls, the countryside could be almost instantly reached by anyone ambulatory.

The practice of planting trees in European cities only began to grow once cities got larger and the countryside grew correspondingly more distant. In the 17th century the great diarist, gardener, and arboriphile John Evelyn visited Antwerp, whose leaders had, half-a-century earlier, planted trees along the whole length of the elevated city walls. "There was nothing about this City," Evelyn rhapsodized, "which more ravished me than those delicious shades and walks of stately Trees, which render the incomparably fortified Works of the Town one of the sweetest places in Europe." He was equally ravished by Amsterdam, where lindens had been planted along the length of the city's canals: of one canalside street he exclaimed, "It appears to be a City in a Wood" — the exact phrase that another traveler of the time used to describe the English town of Norwich. So the presence of many trees in an urban environment was still, then, a source of wonderment.

(Evelyn published in 1664 a compendious tome called *Sylva, or a Discourse of Forest Trees.* This became an enormously popular book in England, and for several generations the definitive guide to native trees. Maggie Campbell-Culver's *A Passion for Trees: The Legacy of John Evelyn* is a beautifully illustrated revisiting of Evelyn's famous guide. But Evelyn was not just interested in native plants: on his travels to the Netherlands he noticed a curious and beautiful flower and picked up a few bulbs to bring back to the great garden he was building at Sayes Court, his estate in Deptford, Kent, on the south bank of the Thames. Evelyn was therefore, more than any other single person, responsible for introducing tulips to England, where they soon created a kind of mania, with tulip societies springing up all over the country. Campbell-Culver reports that Evelyn's great garden fell into disrepair soon after his death, and that nothing of it remains today with the possible exception of a single mulberry tree. This is very sad, but there is consolation from Anna Pavord's remarkable work of social history, *The Tulip:* of the hundreds of tulip societies that once dotted England, only one remains, the Wakefield and North of England Tulip Society, in Yorkshire, and some of the marvelous specimens grown by those gifted amateurs even today are descended from the very bulbs that Evelyn brought from Holland three hundred and fifty years ago.)

Lawrence shows how different cities in Europe — and, later, in America — incorporated trees into their plans. Such plans varied greatly, from the grand boulevards of Paris to the tree-filled residential squares of London. (I am particularly fond of the latter model, which you can see followed in a lovely way in Chicago's Washington Square Park, the city's oldest. The Newberry Library sits on the north side of the square, and one of the great delights of using that excellent library involves sitting at a table and gazing through tall windows at the park's trees. Of course, this means that you don't get much work done and feel guilty later, but life consists mainly of such tradeoffs.) But it took a surprisingly long time to achieve consensus on the validity of tree-planting in cities. As late as 1771, after many of the great London squares had already been built, the anonymous author of a polemic called *Critical Observations on the Buildings and Improvements of London* wrote, icily, "A garden in a street is not less absurd than a street in a garden; and he that wishes to have a row of trees before his door in town, betrays almost as false a taste as he that would build a row of houses for an avenue" — that is, instead of an avenue of trees — "to his seat in the country."

But this poor critic was fighting a losing, indeed a lost, battle. By the nineteenth century it had been agreed, in most cities of the world, that trees are both beautiful and health-giving, and that therefore trees should be planted anywhere in our cities where it is possible to plant them. As we still do.

London's arboriphobic pundit was concerned that the presence of trees interferes with the well-being of people — their aesthetic well-being, anyway — but the modern conservationist takes the opposite position: that the presence of people interferes with the well-being of trees. As Oliver Rackham notes, much conservationist thinking takes as its starting-point an idealized image of woodlands untouched by humanity — the true "wildwood." This ideal is especially problematic, Rackham argues, in places like Europe where human habitation goes back a long way. He quotes from a conservationist who lamented, early in the 20th century, that by the 15th century human beings had cut down most of the primeval forests of Britain; which is true, Rackham says, if he meant the 15th century B.C. It is not clear to Rackham why a state of affairs that pertained three or four thousand years ago should become the norm against which all other times are measured. Why not — this is my thought, not Rackham's — why not long for a still earlier time, the last great period of global cooling, when much of what would later be covered by trees was covered instead by ice?

Rackham's second complaint about modern conservationism stems from his first. If having more trees is always better, then, so the logic goes, they should be planted everywhere. Only by creating vast forests to replace the natural forests we have cut down can we compensate for our previous foolishness. Rackham quotes one of the earliest proponents of this view: "Truly, the waste, and destruction of our Woods, has been so universal, that I conceive nothing less than an universal Plantation of all the sorts of trees will supply, and well encounter [that is, remedy] the defect." Who was this pioneering reformer? Why, John Evelyn, of course — who else? Evelyn seems to have known enough about trees to carry out his scheme, insofar as he could, in thoughtful and reasonable ways, which is more than Rackham can say for many modern conservationists. The problem is that some patches of open ground that look like ideal sites for plantations are poor environments for trees of any kind; or it happens that the trees human beings tend to enjoy are poor choices for the environments in which we place them. Rackham takes a kind of ironic satisfaction in seeing these plantations fail, especially since when they come to be neglected or forgotten, as often happens, the various species that truly belong there gradually drift in and make themselves at home.

"Conservationists," says Rackham, "have a record of trying to play God and rectifying God's mistakes as well as humanity's. Often they make woods fit a predetermined theory (which theory depends on how long ago they were at college) rather than listening to the woods and discovering what each wood has to contribute to conservation as a whole." It's now well-understood that the most catastrophic of these attempts at God-playing was the practice — very common throughout the 20th century, especially in North America and in Brazil, and not yet everywhere rejected — of trying to eradicate forest fires. This over-zealousness deprives woodland ecosystems of the vital benefits of occasional burning, and, worse, insures that when fires do start they find so much combustible material that they become superfires, with dire consequences for forests and people alike.

It's interesting to see that people who love trees and know them intimately, as opposed to those who have merely general instincts for conservation, tend not to erect ideological barriers between the human world and "Nature." Rackham's deeply committed but pragmatic and non-ideological approach credits woodlands with a remarkable ability to manage themselves, and sees a great deal of wisdom in many of our ancient practices of woodcraft — practices formulated when we couldn't dominate our environment and so had to learn to be stewards of it. (There's a picture in *Woodlands* of Rackham slicing a length of oak into radial planks with a froe. Don't know what a froe is? Join the club.) But stewardship of an environment, let us make no mistake, is use — respectful use, with a view toward leaving something for our children to use, and to teach their children to use in turn. So also Colin Tudge, who regrets careless and ruthless exploitation of woodlands as much as anyone could, rejects the hands-off approach as an alternative. He would like to see, for instance, a far greater reliance on wood as a building material, and not just for residential purposes: "although it requires energy to turn a tree trunk into a finished beam, . . . it takes roughly twelve times as much to make a steel girder that is functionally equivalent." And while "timber burns, of course," it's also true that "steel, when overheated, buckles." In just a few pages Tudge makes a surprisingly strong case for a greener architecture, even for commercial buildings, based on timber.

And his thoughts go far beyond this. For instance, Tudge imagines trees as a much greater source of food than they are commonly thought to be — an especially attractive thought given trees' ability to hold soil in place and to moderate climate. In the final pages of his book Tudge grows rhapsodic in an almost Evelyn-like way: it is "marvelously and encouragingly" true that "societies can build their entire economies around trees: economies that are much better for people at large, and infinitely more sustainable, than anything we have at present. Trees could indeed stand at the heart of all the world's economics and politics, just as they are at the center of all terrestrial ecology." I'm not sure whether I believe fully in Tudge's visionary ideal, but I want to. It's a beautiful thing.

Meanwhile, back on my sunporch, I continue to be blessed by the trees around me — even if some of them are probably not ideally suited to the local soil and climate. Maples tend to do very well, though, including the one I spend much of my time staring at. And just the other day, when I was going through some old bills and receipts, I found the report of an arborist we had hired a few years ago to take down a couple of dead trees and trim some others. The crew chief had, helpfully, listed each of our trees by species, and with a slightly accelerated heartbeat I sought the answer to my old question. Turns out that my Tree of Mystery is . . . a silver maple. Oh, like I needed *him* to tell me that.

Gardening and Governing

JUST IN THE center of *Richard II,* Shakespeare's most geometrically designed play, and the only one written wholly in verse, we are presented with a scene in a garden. Richard's Queen and her ladies stroll in it, but are heavy of heart — the King's grip on the throne is quickly loosening — and when the gardener and his servant arrive to do some work, they hide themselves and listen. The gardener offers these instructions:

> Go thou, and like an executioner,
> Cut off the heads of too fast growing sprays,
> That look too lofty in our commonwealth:
> All must be even in our government.

And if this political allegory were not explicit enough, the servant dispenses with it and makes his commentary direct:

> Why should we in the compass of a pale
> Keep law and form and due proportion,
> Showing, as in a model, our firm estate,
> When our sea-walled garden, the whole land,
> Is full of weeds, her fairest flowers choked up,
> Her fruit-trees all unpruned, her hedges ruin'd,
> Her knots disorder'd and her wholesome herbs
> Swarming with caterpillars?

At this point the gardener reveals that "the wasteful king" has been "seized" by Henry Bolingbroke. He exclaims, "O, what pity is it / That he had not so trimm'd and dress'd his land / As we this garden!"

The link between gardening and ruling was not first forged here, but rarely had it been made so strong; and Shakespeare offers the added lovely complication of placing this scene centrally, like a sculpture or tableau at the heart of a formal garden, thereby exhibiting his own skills at design, his own mastery of the available resources.

Gardening marks, as clearly as any activity, the joining of nature and culture. The gardener makes nothing, but rather gathers what God has made and shapes it into new and pleasing forms. The well-designed garden shows nature more clearly and beautifully than nature can show itself. And this can be a model of politics: people left to their own devices can run riot, make themselves and their environment "ruin'd" and "disorder'd"; properly governed, though, they can flourish, they can become their best selves and make the most of their environment.

But the governor's hand, like the gardener's, can fall too heavy. If we grant that Richard has been careless and thoughtless, has failed to govern, has allowed weeds to overwhelm "our sea-walled garden," we may also suspect this gardener, who is quick to appoint an "executioner" and is perhaps overly enamored with "evenness" in his realm. We need governors as we need gardeners; but not all forms of government are equally wise or equally beautiful.

These are among the themes of Tim Richardson's delightfully expansive book *The Arcadian Friends: Inventing the English Landscape Garden*. Richardson explores in apt detail the most eventful and meaning-rich period of English landscape gardening, from the Glorious Revolution of 1688 — during which the English and the Dutch collaborated in governing and gardening alike — to the middle of the next century, when Lancelot "Capability" Brown strode onto the scene and made an impression that still dominates our sense of the English-made landscape.

Brown's nickname came from his habit of scanning a rich man's estate and proclaiming that the place had "capabilities." This was Brown's way of announcing that his task was to work with the existing character of a place, to take advantage of the capabilities it already and natively possessed rather than imposing a purely human vision upon it. Brown's landscapes are cunningly and carefully designed, above all in their apparent lack of design. The visitor to, say, Blenheim Palace who is unaware of these matters is likely to look from the house over the vast rolling grounds and think, "Yes, I can see why someone decided to build a great house here." But the house was built fifty years before Brown showed up; and when he did show up, he planted trees, created hills and valleys, and even dammed a stream to create a little lake, which had the effect of lowering a stone bridge that Brown (rightly) thought was too prominent, distracting from the "natural" beauty of the place. One rival commented that Brown's designs "differ very little from common fields, so closely is nature copied in most of them," which was not meant as a compliment, but Brown surely would have taken it as one.

Brown's designs take us a long, long way from the gardens of the Italian and French Renaissance, which by contrast seem overwhelmingly geometrical and symmetrical — like *Richard II* — and which emphasize the power of art to transform nature. Thus their great reliance on topiary (than which nothing could be more repulsive to Capability Brown). Richardson's purpose is to explain how, in a period of about sixty years, English landscaping got from the old French-Italian model to its opposite. And that explanation begins in the years following the Restoration of the English monarchy in 1660.

When Parliament invited Charles II to assume the throne that he had always thought was rightfully his anyway, they meant for him to understand that the role of king was, from then on, a circumscribed one. Charles got the message — as long as he had his money and his mistresses he was happy enough, and willing to keep his Catholicism under wraps — but his brother and successor James II was somewhat pricklier and more ambitious, and more devoted to his religion. This led leaders of Parliament to begin the negotiations with William of Orange that would lead to James evacuating the throne in 1688 and his being replaced by William and his wife Mary. Among the consequences of this event was a cross-pollination of English and Dutch landscaping styles. Members of the emerging pro-Parliament party, the Whigs, were especially eager to show their support for the alliance with Holland by mimicking the less formal, less elaborate landscapes preferred by the leading lights of that nation.

Moreover, it did not take people long to discern obvious links between styles of governance and styles of gardening. The French and Italian style of shaping nature to art's needs struck many English observers as perfectly consonant with authoritarian monarchial government and the rigid hierarchies of Catholicism. They saw, by contrast, the humbler and more naturalistic style of the Dutch as an echo of deliberative republicanism and the relative egalitarianism of the Protestant faith. So for many aristocrats, gentlemen, and rising merchants, the design of one's garden became a primary way to indicate one's political allegiances.

The Whigs, Richardson demonstrates, were the first to get on board with this program; it took the Tories a while to start playing the game, and even longer to figure out styles of landscaping that would distinguish them from the Whigs without making them seem unpatriotically attached to the ways of England's old enemy France. (They decided to copy the newfangled preference for "wiggling walks" and groves rather than the straight lines and formal parterres of old.) But gradually the rival styles began to emerge. Richardson is quick to say that few of the differences would be apparent to modern eyes, since none of the estates and gardens of that time went nearly as far in the naturalistic direction as Capability Brown would later go; but they were quite evident to people of the time.

Richardson also gives a vivid picture of just how important landscaping became in the aesthetics of 18th-century Europe. Describing the first decade of that century, he writes, "It probably sounds absurd to twenty-first-century ears, attuned to the concept of gardens and gardening as a simple-minded, outdoor version of DIY, but for four decades from this point garden design constituted the cutting edge of international avant-garde art, with Britain leading the way." Thus it makes sense that gardens and landscapes would be the continual objects of attention by the literati of the time. Indeed, the essayist and poet Joseph Addison became something like the Minister of Propaganda, Gardening Division for the Whigs, just as (a little later) Alexander Pope came to perform a similar function for the Tories. They were the great theorists of landscape of their time.

And they were also gardeners themselves, Addison in a belated and offhand way, Pope in a passionate and even obsessive one. Pope's little estate on the Thames in Twickenham — he managed to buy it thanks to subscriptions to his translation of Homer, which made him rich — became the poet's laboratory of design, featuring a tunnel under a road, a tiny temple, statues with classical verses attached to them, and (wonder of wonders) a mineral-encrusted grotto featuring a camera obscura. Pope dearly loved his grotto, and though only a fragment of his design remains, he would be comforted by the knowledge that the grotto is that fragment. Richardson argues that in his over-exuberance Pope tried to cram too much into too little space, and that the resultant busyness compromised the aesthetic effect of the garden, but he is also ready to forgive Pope for that because the Twickenham garden achieved what Richardson believes to be the two great virtues of a garden: variety and individuality.

What Richardson loves above all about the gardens of this period is the way that their owners strove to create botanical and arboreal mirrors of themselves and their interests. In some cases those interests were strongly political, usually represented in statuary: Richardson offers a detailed description of Stowe House in Buckinghamshire, where Lord Cobham built a Temple of British Worthies to identify his heroes, and to mark his villains by omission. But in other cases — notably the magnificent Stourhead in Wiltshire, owned by the Hoares, a banking family — the impulse was thoroughly non-political, rather aesthetic or narrative: the visitor to Stourhead was (and still is) guided through a sequence of widely varying and constantly surprising sights. Statues are hidden in dark grottoes, overhung by dense evergreens; then the visitor emerges from a close tunnel of greenery onto a sudden vista of a lake and, wonderfully, the Pantheon on the far bank, half-encircled by trees. It's like a painting by Poussin, and indeed was designed to give just that effect.

Classical — or more specifically Palladian — buildings like Stourhead's Pantheon were common features on the larger estates, but there were also many kinds of pseudo-temple, the aforementioned grottoes, and, increasingly as the century wore on, hermitages. Usually the hermitages would contain statues or books, but it was sometimes thought that hermitages should be inhabited. Curiously, this becomes a major theme in Tom Stoppard's magnificent 1995 play *Arcadia,* during which Lady Croom hires a bumbling landscape designer named Noakes, whom she comes to refer to as "Culpability" Noakes. When Noakes tells her that he is building a hermitage, and she inquires where he plans to get a hermit, he stammers — not having considered this point — that he could perhaps advertise in the newspaper for one. To this Lady Croom replies, "But surely a hermit who takes a newspaper is not a hermit in whom one can have complete confidence."

A wonderful scene, and we learn from Richardson that it's not wholly fictional. The Hon. Charles Hamilton, in the course of creating what would become one of the masterpieces of the age at his estate Painshill, in Surrey, actually did advertise in the newspapers for a hermit to live in his hermitage. He offered said hermit not only (a very small) room and (meager) board but the princely sum of 700 guineas — about $50,000 — upon certain strict conditions: for seven years the hermit could not shave, cut his hair, trim his fingernails, or speak to anyone. On the plus side, he would receive a hermit's cloak, a human skull, and a Bible. Hamilton got a taker soon enough, and was quite pleased until — just three weeks into the experiment — the hermit was found carousing in a nearby pub and was fired on the spot. Thus confirming the wisdom of Lady Croom's suspicions.

In the great variety of design and ornamentation in the gardens of this age, one notable absence was religion. This led many pious believers to see the increasing popularity among the wealthy of landscape gardening as a sign of encroaching paganism. But Richardson offers a more plausible explanation: the scars of the previous century's religious wars were still fresh enough that few if any landowners were willing to risk the creation of religious symbols that could be misinterpreted, could become flashpoints for anger or resentment. Better to stay on the safe (secular) side.

Richardson gives vivid portraits of these gardens and of the personalities that made or commissioned them: above all Pope, but also Henrietta Howard, the resourceful and charming mistress of George II; the self-effacing genius William Kent, the greatest designer of his age; the energetic Lord Burlington, to whom Pope wrote a great verse epistle; and many more. Almost all of these figures died in the decade or so around 1750, and for Richardson, this date marked the end of the most vivid and exciting period of English landscape design — in part because it also marks the rise of Capability Brown. Brown, Richardson acknowledges, was a great genius, but he employed the same naturalistic ideas — the same irregularly shaped lakes, the same artlessly scattered clumps of trees, the same ha-ha's, the same pastures that came right up to the houses themselves — pretty much everywhere, and the overwhelming popularity of those ideas tended to dampen, if not eliminate, the variety and individuality that had reigned in the first half of the century. Brown's designs were impeccably and subtly tasteful, but Richardson makes a compelling case that impeccable taste isn't everything. The age of the Arcadian Friends was one in which a landscape garden could look like almost anything and have almost anything in it. Richardson misses that age — especially since so few traces of it remain today — and he causes the reader to miss it too.

Blessed Are the Green of Heart

SOME YEARS ago I was leading a summer study tour in Oxford, England, during which as a matter of course — we were from Wheaton College, after all — we paid a visit to Magdalen College, the longtime academic home of C. S. Lewis. The dean of divinity, as Magdalen terms its chaplain, was gracious and welcoming and gave us an informative tour that concluded in the chapel with Morning Prayer. It was lovely in every way, but then at the end something unusual happened. The dean, instead of pronouncing the traditional benediction, began to recite the concluding paragraph of the final adventure in Narnia, *The Last Battle:* "And as He spoke He no longer looked to them like a lion. . . ."

I was reminded recently of the feelings I had on that occasion. It happened when I picked up *The Green Bible*. What is *The Green Bible?* Let the project's website speak for itself:

The Green Bible **includes**
the following distinctive features:

- Green-letter edition: Verses and passages that speak to God's care for creation highlighted in green
- Contributions by Brian McLaren, Matthew Sleeth, N. T. Wright, Desmond Tutu, and many others
- A green Bible index and personal study guide
- Recycled paper, using soy-based ink with a cotton/linen cover

And there's more! Other featured luminaries include John Paul II — strange that he wasn't among the headliners (beaten out by Matthew Sleeth) — and St. Francis of Assisi and Wendell Berry, whose poems serve as epigraphs. Plus, there's an anthology of "Teachings on Creation Through the Ages" that takes us from Clement of Rome to Rick of Saddleback.

Now, before I try to account for my discomfort, I wish it known that my family owns only one car (a six-year-old, four-cylinder Subaru), lives in a house with only one bathroom, and recycles fanatically. I walk to and from work most days and fly rarely. My carbon footprint is perhaps one ten-thousandth the size of Al Gore's. Moreover — and if this does not confirm my bona fides nothing will — I am even now writing a book called *The Gospel of the Trees*. If you're looking for someone greener than me, your only options are the Incredible Hulk and Kermit the Frog.

For that matter, *The Green Bible* has the great merit of treating a theme that is actually in Scripture. The quotation from Romans 8 on the project's homepage — "For the creation waits with eager longing for the revealing of the children of God; for the creation was subjected to futility, not of its own will but by the will of the one who subjected it, in hope that the creation itself will be set free from its bondage to decay and will obtain the freedom of the glory of the children of God" — really is central to the biblical picture of redemption and really has been neglected in both theory and practice. And I may also affirm my nearly boundless admiration not just for John Paul II, St. Francis, and Wendell Berry but for the claims they make in these pages.

But all that said, *The Green Bible* makes me distinctly uncomfortable, just as the dean of divinity did when he invoked dear old C. S. Lewis at the conclusion of Morning Prayer. Lewis is indeed dear to me and to millions of others, but admiration of Lewis is not a prerequisite for participating in the rites of the Church. One could believe that Lewis was a theologically idiotic, reactionary old misogynist who couldn't write his way out of a wet paper bag, whose Narnia tales are a disgraceful blight on the landscape of children's literature, whose Aslan is a blasphemous parody of Our Lord, and — believing all that — one could *still* be a faithful Christian, even a devoted Anglican. To include Lewis's words in worship, as part of the liturgy itself, is to suggest that those words deserve the same reverence that we grant to the Book of Common Prayer and perhaps — given the usual source of liturgical benedictions — Scripture itself.

Now, if the dean had given a homily and in that homily had quoted Lewis, I would have no cause for complaint. Nor, I believe, would the person who loathes Lewis. That person would surely acknowledge (even if wincing while doing so) that preachers, in attempting to interpret Scripture and guide the faithful, are free to draw on a variety of resources to make their points, and that such attempts will not always please everyone. Likewise, a collection of the essays that preface *The Green Bible,* coupled perhaps with an anthology of relevant portions of Scripture, would surely have been a useful and valuable thing. But subjecting the whole of Scripture to one agenda — enfolding it in the single adjective *green* — is, I think, an ill-judged strategy for pursuing a worthwhile goal.

Still more ill judged is the over-egging of the rhetorical pudding. The project website tells us that "with over 1,000 references to the earth in the Bible, compared to 490 references to heaven and 530 references to love, the Bible carries a powerful message for the earth." I am not sure what to make of this *argumentum ad arithmeticum,* unless the point is that the earth is approximately 1.88 times more important to God than love and 2.04 times more important than heaven. Based on my own research into this topic and following the same method, I am prepared to say that the earth is 7.04 times more important to God than donkeys (which are mentioned 142 times in the Bible).

The Green Bible presents us with a curious kind of natural theology: We start with things we know to be true from trusted sources — Al Gore, perhaps? — and then we turn to Scripture to measure it against those preexisting and reliable authorities. And what a relief to discover that God is green. Because we already know that it's good to be green — what we didn't know is whether God measures up to that standard.

The essays in *The Green Bible* teach more or less the same message in varying ways. There's a great deal of overlap to them, and several could easily be discarded, though that would compromise the ecumenical message: We got Catholics, evangelicals, mainliners, Jews, the whole shebang. That message is built around three doctrines: creation

(God made the world and declared it good), stewardship (God gave us the responsibility to care for that creation), and restoration (God's plan is to restore the creation).

Everything else is said to follow from these three essential points. For example, "All the elements of creation . . . are interdependent" (says the unsigned preface) "in such a way that our actions can have repercussions for creatures we will never see." And thus we must "evaluate our *personal consumption* and . . . become free of the idea that our worth and fulfillment are wrapped up in our possessions," as the essay by Gordon Aeschliman puts it.

Moreover, "the poor and vulnerable are members of God's family and are the most severely affected" by environmental disturbances created by other human beings, especially the wealthy, as Archbishop Desmond Tutu claims. This is repeated so frequently, by so many commentators, that it often seems that being green is a secondary good, something we should practice primarily because it helps the poor, with benefits to the earth being a kind of bonus. I am not complaining about this merging of values — it is right to note that Scripture often presents us with networks of virtues and mutually reinforcing practices. But the confluence does raise the question of why this is a *Green* Bible rather than, say, a *Justice* Bible. Could it be that greenness is a sexier commodity right now than justice or peaceableness?

There is one more step that the essays in *The Green Bible* often take, a step into the realm of practical specificity and policy recommendations. Throughout the essays are scattered references to everything from ozone depletion to recycling strategies to the effects of American pet shops on the population of parrots in New Guinea — and recommendations of particular courses of action: Aeschliman's commendation of conservancy strategies, for instance, through which churches purchase endangered land to ensure preservation.

The presence of such policy-oriented commentary raises an interesting question: How do we get from highly general biblical principles to specific policies and practices? For get there we must. The contributors to *The Green Bible* say over and over again that we must act righteously toward, not just think correctly about, creation, and this is surely true. In fact, almost all of their general principles are surely true, so anodynely beyond question that one wonders why they are worth reasserting at such length. Is anyone really going to say, "No, I think my value as a Christian and a human being *is* determined by the number of possessions I have"? Or, "I see no biblical mandate for caring for the poor"? The principles are tiresomely belabored, but the specific policy recommendations don't follow straightforwardly from the principles. How do we get from "We must be good stewards of creation" to "Our church needs to invest in the Eden Conservancy Project"?

It seems to me that one way we get there is through deep and serious empirical study, so that we can determine with some reasonable degree of confidence whether the Eden Conservancy Project — and the general conservation strategy it represents — really is a good way for those of us who want to care for God's creation to invest our resources.

But, of course, any answer to such empirical questions will depend on how well we have formulated the questions — how well we understand our goals and desires, how well we understand our concepts of care and conservation. This is another way of saying that we also must get from general biblical principles or commandments to specific practices through theology.

Alas, there is precious little actual theology going on in *The Green Bible*'s essays, and some of what goes on is, shall we say, inadvertent: The preface tells us that "God and Jesus interact with, care for, and are intimately involved with all of creation." (God *and* Jesus? Remarkable. But only the two of them?) N. T. Wright's largely exegetical essay "Jesus Is Coming — Plant a Tree!" is surely the most theologically deep and intellectually provocative item in the bunch. Even the address by John Paul II is theologically thin, largely because it was given to commemorate the World Day of Peace in 1990 and was therefore directed to a general audience.

But even if the theology here were rich and deep and uniformly brilliant, I would still be concerned about a Bible with so much ancillary material on a single subject. This strategy too easily conflates a particular agenda and the whole biblical message. If God is green, then are the green also godly? The essays in *The Green Bible* don't do anything to discourage that line of thought.

But what about the text of Scripture itself? This is after all a "green-letter edition," in which "verses and passages that speak to God's care for creation" are "highlighted in green." I cannot help being reminded of a gift I received about thirty years ago, the *Salem Kirban Bible*. Salem Kirban was a biblical-prophecy guru who flourished in the 1970s — think of a minor-league Hal Lindsey — who produced a Bible in which every passage of Scripture relating to the end times was highlighted, magnified, commented on, and surrounded by illustrations. Meanwhile the rest of Scripture was consigned to unreadably small type, as befitted the *adiaphora* contained within it.

Well, *The Green Bible* is not quite so bad: The text may be green or black, but it's all the same size. Still, the greenness, along with the "Green Bible Trail Guide" at the back of the book, does say pretty clearly, "This is the stuff that really matters," which is another way of saying, "That other, nonemphasized stuff doesn't matter as much." And in that sense this project isn't all that different from the *Salem Kirban Bible*. Green is the new dispensationalism, I suppose.

It may be asked at this point whether I also protest the existence of red-letter Bibles, with their singling out of the words of Jesus, as though those have greater authority than the rest of the Bible. Well, to be truthful, I do, rather, and therefore I'm not sanguine about Tony Campolo's "red-letter Christian" movement, with its claim to give particular emphasis to the (supposedly neglected) words of Jesus. But Campolo at least makes the theologically responsible argument that "you can only understand the rest of the Bible when you read it from the perspective provided by Christ."

Reading the Bible "from the perspective provided by" the green letters doesn't work that way. For Christians, Jesus Christ is not only the Way, the Truth, and the Life. He is also, as St. Paul says, the end of the Law and its fulfillment: "He is the image of the invisible God, the first-born of all creation. For by him all things were created, in heaven and on earth, visible and invisible, whether thrones or dominions or rulers or authorities — all things were created through him and for him." Nothing of the kind can be said for the green-letter themes. Christ leads you to everything else; greenness does not. And the green lettering invites us to separate one theme from others, extracting it from the larger story of which it is a part.

Is it fair to ask *The Green Bible* to make all these theological connections? Yes, because it's a complete Bible. The green lettering, the prefatory essays, and the concluding study guide collectively suggest that this one theme is the interpretative key to all of Scripture. And that's simply not a sustainable claim.

This would be true even if the green-lettered verses presented a clear and consistent message, but they do not. Many of them say what you might expect them to say, but others can be irrelevant or disturbing. The irrelevant ones come when the editors are stretching too far to make a point, something that happens especially in the Gospels, presumably from a desire to enlist Jesus in the cause. It's hard to think of any other reason why this passage would be printed in green: "In the morning, when it was still very dark, he got up and went out to a deserted place, where he prayed." And what precisely is green about "Do not judge, and you will not be judged; do not condemn, and you will not be condemned"?

The disturbing selections — which, to give the editors full credit, are faithfully green-lettered — suggest that the whole idea of "God's care for creation" is far more complex than our usual pieties indicate. What are we to do with, for instance, these words from Ezekiel? "Mortal, set your face towards the south, preach against the south, and prophesy against the forest land in the Negeb; say to the forest of the Negeb, Hear the word of the Lord: Thus says the Lord God, I will kindle a fire in you, and it shall devour every green tree in you, and every dry tree; the blazing fire shall not be quenched, and all faces from south to north shall be scorched by it."

We are perhaps not as awed as the first audience of the book of Job might have been by God's invocation of Leviathan and Behemoth — we can see such creatures in the zoo — but this picture of God as the agent of pure destruction, as the divine arsonist, is surely unsettling. Even Jesus curses and blights a fig tree, and, while he may have done so to make a point about human beings, it was the fig tree that paid the price.

Some will argue that the book of Revelation promises the complete destruction of this world and its replacement by "a new heaven and a new earth." I am not inclined to that view; I tend to agree with N. T.

Wright that the vision points to a moment when the new creation is made "not *ex nihilo,* but *ex vetere,* not out of nothing, but out of the old one, the existing one," just as the resurrected body of Jesus is not a brand-new body but his old one glorified.

Even so, we must face the fact that God's interaction with his creation is not always constructive and restorative but is often shockingly destructive. It is true that the destruction always precedes some kind of renewal, but it is destruction all the same, and while we can come up with comforting scenarios in which we do the same kind of thing — controlled burns in forest management and farming, for instance — it would be best not to allegorize too readily. God loves his creation, but he deals with it in ways that, to us, are sometimes indistinguishable from hatred. As he deals with us.

Our explanations for all this often come perilously close to explaining it away. I would be inclined to give *The Green Bible* only to those who have passed a detailed examination on the book of Job, about the end of which G. K. Chesterton wisely said, "The riddles of God are more satisfying than the solutions of man."

I would guess that *The Green Bible* is addressed to two constituencies. First, committed environmentalists, or those at least deeply attracted to it, who view Christianity with skepticism; people who might become more open to Christianity if they come to believe that God is green. And second, Christians who would like to find some biblical warrant for their attraction to environmental issues. Members of each group *could* benefit from this book, but only if they are able to maintain a critical distance from some of its claims, implicit and explicit.

How many such people are there? I couldn't say. But it is worth noting that, in a recent Pew Forum survey of the political priorities of white evangelicals, the environment came in next-to-last in importance. (The only lower priority among the thirteen on the list was gay marriage; the economy led the pack.) Results for "white non-Hispanic Catholics" were roughly similar.

Meanwhile, in Lake Superior State University's annual "List of Words to Be Banished from the Queen's English for Misuse, Overuse, and General Uselessness" — tabulated from readers' submissions — *green* has just come in first. "I'm all for being environmentally responsible, but this *green* needs to be nipped in the bud," says Valerie Gilson of Gales Ferry, Connecticut, employing an apt idiom. The more vigorous Ed Hardiman of Bristow, Virginia, says, "If I see one more corporation declare itself *green,* I'm going to start burning tires in my backyard."

So it's possible that *The Green Bible* is actually poised between two audiences: one unready for the message, one already tired of it. Meanwhile, the creation, still "subjected to futility," continues to "wait with eager longing" to be "set free from its bondage to decay." And we, even at our best, still strive to know what it means to hold this world in stewardship. *Creation* remains always too large for us, too abstract. What's real is this furrow of black soil, that crabapple tree: These we can protect insofar as we see them, touch them, and therefore know them. But no general principle, no notion of greenness, can tell us how to care for what occupies our field of vision this moment, what sifts between our outstretched fingers.

The End of Friendship

SAMUEL JOHNSON had a great gift for friendship, and exercised it consistently. But he also knew that friendships do not always last, that they change, that they fade. Perhaps a man with many friends is best situated to understand this mutability. In a sober essay from *The Idler*, he writes, "The most fatal disease of friendship is gradual decay, or dislike hourly increased by causes too slender for complaint, and too numerous for removal. — Those who are angry may be reconciled; those who have been injured may receive a recompense; but when the desire of pleasing and willingness to be pleased is silently diminished, the renovation of friendship is hopeless; as, when the vital powers sink into languor, there is no longer any use of the physician."

Why are friendships so readily susceptible to these dangers? Why are they at the mercy of contingency? I believe it is because they have no end, no *telos,* other than their own continuation. The contingency that Johnson noted in the commencement of a friendship remains active throughout the relationship's course: how well a bond is sustained, indeed whether it is sustained at all, is something that accident determines. As Johnson notes, friendship is a matter largely of mutual pleasure, the pleasure of one another's company, and when pleasure fades, it fades. The former friends may still see one another; they may be cordial; they may in a serious sense love one another. If they are Christians they may cherish the bond they have as brothers or sisters in Christ. But friendship as such will be over.

128

I take it that this, or something like it, is what happened to C. S. Lewis and J. R. R. Tolkien, who were at one time the most intimate of friends. Tolkien always said that he would not have finished *The Lord of the Rings* without Lewis's support ("The unpayable debt that I owe to him was not 'influence' as it is ordinarily understood, but sheer encouragement") and when Lewis died he wrote, "This feels like an axe-blow near the roots." I don't think there was ever a time when the two men did not love each other; but their friendship had ended at least a dozen years before Lewis's death. Tolkien had to learn of Lewis's marriage to Joy Davidman long after it happened and from a third party.

Biographers — I among them — have tried to understand the circumstances that led to the separation of the two men. Such matters are partially comprehensible, and mostly involve Tolkien's frustrations with Lewis, who was (for Tolkien's taste) too fluent a writer, too bold a speaker, too ecumenical a Christian, and too miscellaneously acquisitive a thinker. But how these frustrations, and others we are unaware of, came to displace, or overwhelm, the pleasure the two men once had in each other's company — this we cannot know. And I do not mean we cannot know it because the former friends left no records, though indeed they left none that really help. On a deeper level, there is simply no way to describe or even account for the curious internal seismic shifts that lead one person to take less delight in the presence of another, that exacerbate minor irritants until they become primary responses, that see excitement at the thought of a meeting yield to a sense of duty or even the determination to escape. When Tolkien sought to get Lewis a chair at Cambridge, he was indeed utterly convinced that Lewis deserved the honor; but it is hard not to suspect that he looked forward to a day when he and his former intimate were not spending their days just a few hundred feet apart — the distance between Merton and Magdalen colleges — but without ever seeking each other's company. Surely that was an awkwardness — intensified tenfold when they passed each other on High Street, as often they must have — Tolkien was glad to put behind him.

But I speculate. I speculate because the end of a friendship is something mysterious — though, really, no less mysterious than the daily course of a vibrant one. Reading Montaigne's tribute to his deceased friend Etienne de la Boetie in "Of Friendship," one is surprised by how little it says — how little it *can* say — about its supposed topic. Montaigne devotes the first half of the essay to distinguishing friendship from other forms of affection and pointing out relationships that cannot develop into friendship — for instance, those between parents and children. (He is interestingly noncommittal about friendship between men and women, contenting himself with saying that the ancients unanimously denied its possibility; but unanimous testimony of the ancients is usually sufficient to earn warm agreement from Montaigne. Why is that not forthcoming here? We might note here that la Boetie had produced a French version of Plutarch's *Consolation to His Wife* [on the death of a child], and instructed Montaigne to share the work with his friends. Since Montaigne and his wife had just recently lost a child of their own, Montaigne wrote a tender preface to her, and as for friends, he commented, "I have none more intimate than you." So here was one case where his own incontrovertible experience trumped the wisdom of the ancients, even if he did not wish to say so flatly.)

The second half of Montaigne's "Of Friendship" is largely devoted to grief, to Montaigne's declaration of his misery now that la Boetie is gone. So the essay as a whole seems to circle about friendship, saying what it is not, saying how it feels to lose it, but offering scarcely a glimpse of the experience itself. And it is surprising how often this evasiveness afflicts literary representations of friendship. Think of Nisus and Euryalus, whose friendship Virgil in the *Aeneid* says he will cause to be remembered always. We are told *that* they were the greatest of friends, but all we see of them is the kind of cheerful mock-rivalry that companions in arms often share. They are fellow competitors for honor and glory; it is not accidental that we first hear of them as participants in a footrace, in which Nisus, when he stumbles and falls, makes a point of taking out a strong runner so that Euryalus can run ahead to the finish, "a winner / because of his friend's kindness." But the devotion of Nisus could be that of a lover as well as a friend, and indeed in Virgil's statement that Nisus is "known for his love of the youth" Euryalus, who in turn is known for his adolescent good looks — he is the classic *ephebus* — there is every indication that Euryalus is (to borrow the Athenian terms) the *eromenos,* the unique object of romantic affection for Nisus, the older man, the *erastes*. I hope I can say this without awakening the suspicion that, like many literary critics of my generation, I invariably see homoeroticism where the ancients would have seen friendship. I think Virgil gives ample warrant for this suggestion, which in any case is meant only to support my claim that literary treatments of friendship have this strange tendency, when inspected, to transform into something else or evaporate altogether.

Even in *The Lord of the Rings* the male relationships, so beautifully evoked, are seen primarily in the setting of warfare, so that it is hard to distinguish friendship proper from a rather different phenomenon, the peculiarly intense bonds shared by companions in arms. People can become intimate and devoted to one another through shared experiences of war who would never have been friends in another walk of life; this is a common theme in memoirs of war. Though we know that Sam and Frodo, Merry and Pippin are friends in the everyday life of the Shire, we scarcely *see* them in that world; it is as companions in arms that their relationships are developed for us. In that one sense they are like Nisus and Euryalus.

The key to this puzzle, I think, may be found in one of the few comments in Montaigne's "Of Friendship" that speaks directly to his bond with la Boetie. It is the most famous line in the essay: "In the friendship I speak of, our souls mingle and blend with each other so completely that they efface the seam that joined them, and cannot find it again. If you press me to tell why I loved him, I feel that this cannot be expressed, except by answering, Because it was he, because it was I." (In the first version of this essay Montaigne ended the sentence with "this cannot be expressed.") The importance of these sentences for our purposes here can be seen if we turn to a thoughtful, provocative book, M. A. Screech's *Montaigne and Melancholy*.

Screech points out that Montaigne is much concerned througout the *Essays* with *ecstatic* experiences, experiences that take us out of ourselves, beyond the boundaries of selfhood. Melancholy itself is one of those experiences, as are certain kinds of religious consciousness, and of course sexual passion. In fact it is the ecstatic character of sexual passion that leads Montaigne to see it as incompatible with friendship. Screech doesn't have much to say about friendship in his book, precisely because it is the nature of friendship to be un-ecstatic, to bring one back into oneself rather than throw one beyond. Again: "In the friendship I speak of, our souls mingle and blend with each other so completely that they efface the seam that joined them, and cannot find it again." It is a reinforcement, a renewal of the known, a confirmation of its value. The ecstasies have a certain alienating effect, there is something *unheimlich* about them; but friendship is, definitively, *heimlich*, homely, comforting.

Surely ecstasy is the very stuff of literature: to be taken out of ourselves is to have a story to tell, a sequence of events to dramatize, an intensity of experience to lyricize. Might it be that experiences which are the inverse of ecstatic are also and thereby the inverse of literary? Could be that the end (the conclusion) of friendship is the only element of it that is even partially representable, because it marks the *loss* of the *heimlich?* In trying to describe the texture of his friendship with la Boetie Montaigne is driven first to a statement of inexpressibility and then to tautology — "Because it was he, because it was I" — and even in describing the end of friendships Johnson does little better: to draw an analogy to the moment "when the vital powers sink into languor" and "there is no longer any use of the physician" is simply to say that friendships die when they die. But once they *do* die, then the whole vast literary apparatus of grief and loss comes to our aid.

The inexpressibility of friendship is also related, I think, to its non-teleological character, to its having no end save its own perpetuation. Having no specific goal in mind, having nothing to strive towards, friendships possess no intrinsic *narrative* quality. This is not to say that we should not strive to be better friends, that is, to practice more assiduously the virtues that strengthen friendship, but we cannot really strive to be more intimate with a particular friend. At least, we cannot do so for reasons intrinsic to the friendship. It is in the nature of friendship, I think, that the demands a friendship makes upon us wax and wane: we go through seasons of relative closeness, seasons of relative separation, without re-evaluating the basic character of the friendship. (I have dear, dear friends whom I can see only rarely, but they are no less dear because of this, and would be no *more* dear if we could meet regularly.) This stability of affection coupled with great variation in occasions for intimacy is almost impossible to represent in narrative terms, or indeed in other literary terms.

This is a troubling thought for more than one reason. Consider Montaigne's situation, able to describe his grief, but unable to describe the very experience of which he is bereaved. This is yet another aspect of the fragility that Johnson is so aware of: when an experience is beyond our power to depict, once it's over it is doubly lost: we cannot even be consoled by our portrayals of it. Even a bungled romantic affair yields a narrative, something that can be told, reviewed, reconsidered, relived. Think of Hazlitt's *Liber Amoris,* a pathetic tale, but one whose telling gave poor Hazlitt some comfort. Friendships — whether vibrant, weakened, or dead — don't readily yield to such attempts at form-giving. If this doesn't make them more fragile, it certainly makes them feel so.

But there is, as it happens, a literary genre that lends itself to the representation of friendship, at least to a limited degree. It is a genre often neglected, or even forgotten; it has been a long time since anyone took it seriously as a mode of literary art. That genre is the *epistle,* especially in the hands of its greatest practitioner, Quintus Horatius Flaccus, better known to us as Horace.

The epistles of Horace do not represent friendship directly; we have already seen, repeatedly, why that is nearly impossible. But an indirect portrayal, such as Horace offers, suits something distinctive to the experiences of friends, something pointed to by C. S. Lewis in a famous passage from *The Four Loves:* "Lovers are always talking to one another about their love; friends hardly ever about their friendship. Lovers are normally face to face, absorbed in each other; friends, side by side, absorbed in a common interest." Such common interests — the contexts and materials of friends' communion, the *environments* in which love grows — are what we can see in friendship, and what is susceptible of literary treatment. Horace does this better than anyone — which is not surprising, really, given his preference for the mundane and the *heimlich.* I quote from the marvelously poetic, if somewhat elastic, translation of David Ferry:

> My aim is to take familiar things and make
> Poetry of them, and do it in such a way

That it looks as if it was easy as could be
For anybody to do it (although he'd sweat
And strain and work his head off, all in vain).
Such is the power of judgment, of knowing what
It means to put the elements together
In just the right way; such is the power of making
A perfectly wonderful thing out of nothing much.

"A perfectly wonderful thing out of nothing much" — a rather fine description of friendship itself; a still better one of Horace's lines, which always verge on the prosaic without ever losing their sublimely poetic balance and elegance. (In his first poems, the *Satires,* he claimed to be worried that his work was *sermoni propiora,* too prosy, but I think that was just poor-mouthing. From the beginning he knew what he was about.)

The salutations of Horace's verse epistles are key to their development: from the outset a tone is established, a tone of relationship. Here the poet addresses a younger man, lecturing a bit, but affectionately, and with a smile:

While you're in Rome, studying declamation,
Here I am in Praeneste, reading Homer,
From whom we learn more than we learn from Crantor
Or Chrysippus, and learn it more clearly, about
The good and bad of things, what's helpful to know,
What isn't. I'll tell you why I think so, if
You've got the time and willingness to listen.

To his equals he commences in a jauntier tone: "Vala, what's the winter like at Velia? / Tell me about the climate at Salerno. / What are the people like? Are there good roads?"

But of course it is in the epistles to Maecenas — his friend, yes, and truly, but also his patron, the giver of his Sabine farm — that the tone is richest and most complex.

Maecenas, you were the first to be named in the first
Poem I ever wrote and you'll be the first

> To be named in the last I'm ever going to write,
> So why on earth, Maecenas, do you persist
> In trying to send a beat-up old-timer like me
> Back into the ring?

It is quite astonishing to realize how many *notes* of friendship — major chords, minor ones, diminished — are struck and held in these lines. The deferential respect of those first lines yields soon to stubbornness, and then (later in the poem) to an insistence on Horace's part that he knows perfectly well what he's doing in giving up poetry for "the study / Of what is genuine and right for me." Such work, he sternly insists, is "the sort of project that, if carried out / Successfully, is good for anyone."

By the end of the poem Horace has brought himself to give Maecenas something of a lecture. "Maecenas, you notice and laugh if the barber gives me / A crooked haircut" — but you are "perfectly unperturbed"

> when I don't know what my own mind is,
> Hating the thing I just now loved, and wanting
> The thing I just rejected scornfully. . . .

Such "seething and boiling" is unphilosophical, unworthy of what Horace should be, and Maecenas should take note of that and sympathize. After all,

> The wise man's second only to Jupiter:
> He is a king of kings in his own life,
> As the Stoics say; free, beautiful, most honored,
> And above all else he's reasonable and sane,
> Unless, of course, he's got a bad toothache.

How delightfully, then, the lecture is curtailed, with a gentle and self-deprecating joke that re-establishes a casual intimacy. Likewise, in other epistles to Maecenas Horace boasts, confesses his fears, offers further lectures on poetry — taken all together they form as lovely and vivid a picture of a friendship as we have, and as we are likely to get.

For Horace has had few successors in the cultivation of this genre; the major practitioners of the epistle, in English at least, can be ticked off on just a few fingers. Alexander Pope stands alone: has any major poet save Horace himself written so many epistles? Doctor Johnson wrote some, of course, and in our own time Czeslaw Milosz. The epistolary voice is heard often, for those with ears to hear, in Elizabeth Bishop's poems; and more often still in those of the later Auden, who consciously practiced a thoughtful Horatianism, especially in his uncomprehended and virtually unnoticed poetic sequence "Thanksgiving for a Habitat," whose quietly masterful poems occasionally come near to quotation from the master.

Matthew Arnold claimed that Horace "wants seriousness," but Arnold was unable to distinguish the serious from the ecstatic. The quiet humilities of Horace, the quiet humilities of friendship, escaped his eye, trained as it was to look high and far. Horace is willing to forgo the attention of such readers; as D. S. Carne-Ross as written, "A double-dyed ironist, he smilingly collaborates with his own under-reading. . . . His great gift was to make the commonplace notable, even luminous, not to be discarded as the everyday trivia of existence. By putting a shine on our small occasions, he shows that the daily drab need not be as drab as it often is." Who could be better suited to teaching us the "small occasions" that comprise the great good of friendship? Perhaps if we learned to take Horace more seriously we could take those occasions seriously as well — though not with over-solemnity, and not without humor. To make sweet companionship of "nothing much," to learn from one another the art of noticing and treasuring life's small pleasures — surely this, if anything, is the end of friendship.

Do-It-Yourself Tradition

OVER THE past forty years the Christian evangelical movement in America has been branching and forking in interesting ways. Because that movement is rooted in the rise of fundamentalism a hundred years ago, it has tended to emphasize the necessity of sound doctrine, especially regarding the uniqueness of Jesus Christ and the absolute authority of Scripture.

But thanks in part to the work of such scholars as Robert Webber and Thomas Howard, and thanks in part to increasing evangelical fondness for Anglican and Catholic writers, about thirty years ago a subset of these evangelicals began to feel that doctrine was not enough. It was necessary, for evangelicals who wished to be not just doctrinally sound but also spiritually vibrant, to connect with ancient traditions of worship. Almost simultaneously, others were being drawn into the rather different but equally worship-centered traditions of the charismatics and Pentecostals.

Now, many evangelicals — most, I think it's fair to say — did not feel the need to move in either of these directions. But the shifts were nonetheless significant, involving millions of Christians. So evangelicalism grew branches that, while not necessarily neglecting doctrine, place a great emphasis on the centrality of worship to the Christian life.

More recently, we have heard from a third generation of evangelicals for whom worship is not enough either. For them the watchword is *practice* — as in the practices of the Christian life, especially those promoted by venerable, pre-Reformation Christian traditions. This move-ment is related in significant ways to the cultivation of the spiritual dis-ciplines that rose to prominence a couple of decades ago, courtesy of Dallas Willard and Richard Foster; but those who emphasize practices often believe that the disciplines, at least as taught by Willard and Fos-ter, tend to be overly individualistic, focused on personal piety, and dis-connected from communal living.

For these advocates of traditional Christian practices, we need visi-bly different ways of living in the world and with one another. Hugh Halter and Matt Smay call this "incarnational community"; Jonathan Wilson-Hartgrove advocates the slightly more specialized practice that he calls "the new monasticism." Whatever we call it, this movement claims to be both deeply historical and vibrantly contemporary. But it seems likely to me that only one of those claims can be sustained. Thinking historically is hard; acting historically well-nigh impossible — at least here, in America, today.

All you need to know about Halter and Smay's book *The Tangible Kingdom: Creating Incarnational Community* may be this: Their chapter on the history of the Church since the fourth century is called "The 1,700-Year Wedgie." That neatly captures the book's tone and its level of intellectual seriousness. If we can call this an argument, it's a familiar one. From Luther's time to our own, every generation of Protestants produces people who rise up to proclaim that the Church lost its way within decades of Jesus' death, leaving the true gospel forgotten and unproclaimed until . . . well, us.

The perfect image of this attitude may be seen in Philip Yancey's 1995 book *The Jesus I Never Knew,* in which he claims that the Christian Church has consistently obscured the character of the true biblical Lord. Thus the book's cover, on which a hand — presumably Yancey's — wipes away centuries of grime from the pictured face of Jesus so that his coun-tenance is revealed in all its glory. We are obviously meant to think of the restoration of artistic masterpieces, and, indeed, Yancey employs just this metaphor, claiming that at times in the writing of his book he "felt like an art restorer stretched out on the scaffolding of the Sistine Chapel, swabbing away the grime of history with a moistened Q-tip. If I scrub hard enough, will I find the original beneath all these layers?"

The difference between Yancey's book and that of Halter and Smay would seem to be that Yancey sees history only as "grime," while Halter and Smay want to reclaim (as the book's cover has it) "the posture and practices of the ancient church now." But you need a microscope to find references to "the ancient church" in *The Tangible Kingdom*. The book is almost wholly composed of anecdotes and the occasional chart or table. Halter and Smay have read the Acts of the Apostles, and they know that the first Christians cared for one another materially as well as spiritually, and that's what they want us to do. Their constant implication is that "traditional churches" have almost completely neglected this apostolic example.

Halter and Smay would insist that they are not so critical. Their book contains twenty or more statements such as this one: "The point of this discussion is not to judge this traditional Church structure, to call it bad or out of date." But just a few sentences before that particular disclaimer, Halter tells a story about a time when he was preaching and got a biblical fact wrong — oddly, he calls this "an inaccurate theological statement" — only to be corrected by his worship leader, just an instant before he would have corrected himself. He then says, "In many churches, I'd have been fired before the next Sunday for incompetence. In my church, we all just laughed and made the correction as a community and moved on."

Really? Many churches would fire a pastor for a single misstatement that he knew to be a misstatement and was on the verge of correcting? I wonder if there has been a single church in the history of the faith that has done such a thing — but this is the way Halter and Smay consistently present traditional churches: as focused so pedantically and pathologically on intellectual minutiae that they can't recognize the deep "tangible" needs of their own people and of strangers in their midst.

It's clear that Halter and Smay have a genuine zeal for the gospel, and my guess is that they have reached many people for Christ who would never darken the door of a "traditional church." May God bless their work. But neither good hearts nor good works can make a good book out of a very bad one, and nothing here lends credence to their claim to have recovered the priorities of "the ancient church." They don't appear to know anything much about the ancient Church; they certainly aren't aware that the social, economic, and political strategies of that Church varied greatly from one location and period to another; they're simply not serious about their historical judgments. I am not even sure why they go to such pains to claim an attachment to our first Christian ancestors — though that is a question we will need to consider before we're done.

This brings us to Brian McLaren. I should probably pause here to note that McLaren is the man most often named as the leader of the "emergent Church movement," though by this point I am already sick of the "[insert adjective here] Church movement" formulation. The title of his new book, *Finding Our Way Again: The Return of the Ancient Practices,* indicates that he too is engaged in a historical salvage operation, but in this case the indication has more justification.

In many respects McLaren's book resembles *The Tangible Kingdom.* It has the same fondness for sweeping historical generalizations and for charts that are just cleaned-up PowerPoint slides. He tells a lot of stories, some of them about fishing. (All these books may set out prescriptions for changing the world, but one verity they never question is the absolute necessity of having at least one-third of their text taken up by folksy anecdotes.) He has a fondness for sage statements that don't add up to anything discernible. For instance, "Jesus never makes 'Christians' or 'converts,' but he calls disciples and sends them out." Okay — but does this mean that we're not to use the term "Christian"? That we're not supposed to speak of "converts" or "conversion" to "Christianity"? That we're not supposed to use language Jesus didn't use? And if not, then what is the point of this sentence? McLaren never explains.

Also, like Halter and Smay, McLaren tends to disparage mere doctrinal correctness. "We must rediscover our faith as a way of life," he says, "not simply as a system of belief." Now, it's true that many evangelicals have a tendency to focus on right doctrine to the near-exclusion of other aspects of the Christian life, but it's simply unhealthy to respond by minimizing the importance of such doctrine.

McLaren is probably using the word "system" disparagingly, but, if we take that word in a better sense and think of the various affirmations of the creeds as interlocking and mutually reinforcing statements, such that any given affirmation loses some of its force if it is not in proper relation to all the others — well, in that case, the achievement of a genuine system of belief is anything but simple. In lectures and speeches, as well as in his books, McLaren often pauses to say that he really does believe that doctrine is important. But he has to say this because he doesn't otherwise show signs of being interested in it. As far as I can tell, McLaren thinks getting the doctrine right is easy — comparatively speaking, anyway. But the history of Christianity scarcely bears out that confidence.

Certainly orthodoxy is not truly right unless it produces the fruits of virtue, service, and prayer. And while this has always been understood within the Church — it was not Brian McLaren who coined the statement "Faith without works is dead" — we Christians have always been tempted to content ourselves with just part of the picture. McLaren rightly wishes to commend to us the personal and communal practices of a lively Christian faith.

"Missional" is the word he uses for those practices that connect the Church with the world, believers with nonbelievers: "Practicing neighborliness, including towards enemies," "Speaking truth in love," "Giving to the poor," "Proclaiming the good news in word and deed." Some may be inclined to ask, "Those are practices?" And indeed, by halfway through *Finding Our Way Again* you may well wonder what isn't a practice. Fasting, feasting, contemplation, Bible reading, listening, interpreting, singing, being still, serving, confronting evil, speaking and working for justice, showing up on time for church — all these and many more turn up in McLaren's lists, without a word to explain why we would call all these things practices, or how they are to be distinguished from other kinds of acts, or what is particularly ancient about them. (Many of the most ancient ones are ones that we've never stopped doing: Singing, for instance, is not a forgotten practice.)

But then, near the end, McLaren's book takes a curious turn. He asks his readers to imagine themselves cast back into the Middle Ages, as wanderers in a strange land, who then come upon a monastery. The monastery is run by an abbess — you're not looking for historical plausibility here, I trust? — who knows, and is willing to teach to the pilgrims, the ascetic practices of both the Western and Eastern Church traditions. So, under her guidance, we are introduced to *katharsis* (or the *via purgativa*), *fotosis* (or the *via illuminativa*), and *theosis* (or the *via unitiva*). Again, let's not pause to ask whether, say, *theosis* and *via unitiva* really are synonymous — as former President George H. W. Bush used to say, it wouldn't be prudent. And anyway, there are more interesting things afoot here.

First, let's note that this "threefold way" isn't a practice, or set of practices, but rather an overarching scheme that gives us reasons for employing spiritual disciplines. We employ these disciplines so that we can be cleansed of unholy and unhealthy affections, turned toward God, and then united with him in love. It would have been helpful if McLaren had presented this structure at the beginning of the book rather than at the end. That he did not may simply be a testament to his own informal, not to say disorganized, style, or it may be that the evident interiority of the threefold way is itself a problem — for it presumes a person who is devoted to the contemplative life and does not invoke (explicitly, anyway) either the "communal" or the "missional." It would have been difficult for McLaren to shoehorn everything he writes about here into this simple structure.

Few of us are able to live the contemplative life; at most we pursue what in the Middle Ages was sometimes known as the mixed life. Which makes it interesting that, when McLaren introduces the threefold way, he does so by taking us out of our own time and our own forms of living. I think he does this because it is difficult to imagine how we can order our own twenty-first-century American lives according to this pattern.

McLaren, like Halter and Smay, wants to commend to us the wisdom of "the ancient church." Apparently that phrase could refer to the Acts of the Apostles or to a period fourteen hundred years later, but, in any case, the idea is that these long-ago Christians did things that we ought to be doing, with habits of prayer and worship and service that we ought to have. But it is also true that those Christians had very different lives than we have. Even if we think in material terms only, the world of Acts is in almost every way alien to our own; all the monastic movements that arose later demand daily routines that bear little resemblance to ours. These facts do not seem to occur to Halter and Smay, while McLaren's invocation of his fictional abbess suggests that he is aware of them but is unsure what their implications are.

Halter, Smay, and McLaren are all pragmatic people and (to borrow a fancy but useful word from the anthropologist Claude Levi-Strauss) *bricoleurs*. A *bricoleur* is someone who takes up whatever tools are at hand to get a job done. He doesn't worry about consistency or perfect fit but about making progress toward a goal. So McLaren gathers some Anglican liturgy here, some Orthodox ascetic spirituality there, and adds to them a few tricks picked up from Western monastic traditions. Do they all fit together seamlessly? Probably not, but there's something here for everyone, surely. McLaren's model of spirituality seems to be predicated on that most American of phrases: "You've got to find what works for you."

There's a certain urgency to the *bricoleur*. He doesn't have time to step back and get a broad overview of his project; he's got to get moving, to keep moving. But there is also, on another level, a curious kind of fixedness to him. If he is determined to work with "whatever tools are at hand," that means that he's rooted to the spot. He's going to work here. And maybe that's what he has to do.

But then, as we know, some people move. Some people come to believe that they can't get the job done where they are, that, if they are going to pursue what's really important to them, they have to find a different location, a different set of conditions. Some of the people who come to that realization we call monks and nuns, anchorites and hermits. That some of the things a Christian might want or need to do simply cannot be done where we are — or can be done here only by some — is a possibility that McLaren and Halter and Smay never seriously entertain. Their consistent assumption is that American Christians are going to live where and how they currently live, and that any spiritual practices they adopt are going to have to be fit into those pre-existing structures.

But the sense that some practices of Christian disciples are linked to certain forms of life and cannot be developed just anywhere underlies every form of monasticism and retreat from the *saeculum*. Many of the practices that McLaren recommends were formulated by people who had left everyday life precisely in order to devote themselves to those practices. Would a serious abbess think that the lifelong disciplines of her people could simply be transferred to the daily experience of a lawyer or a plumber?

It's an awareness of this potential problem that has prompted a movement with which Jonathan Wilson-Hartgrove associates himself: the "new monasticism." At least, that was the impression I got from the book's cover, so I turned to his account with some hopefulness. And some of that hope was fulfilled — especially in his emphasis on the value of "relocation" — though the movement that Wilson-Hartgrove associates himself with is misnamed: There's nothing new about it, nor is it a form of monasticism.

Wilson-Hartgrove and his family and friends live together in what is sometimes called an "intentional Christian community": a group of people, some married, some unmarried, who all live in the same city neighborhood and agree to practice the Christian faith in the same way. Wilson-Hartgrove is happy to announce his debt to certain great predecessors in this kind of endeavor: the Catholic Worker movement led by Dorothy Day and Peter Maurin, Clarence Jordan's Koinonia Farm in Georgia, and the Bruderhof community, which began in Germany and has now spread elsewhere.

But none of those efforts was new either: Nineteenth-century America was full of such communities, as was eighteenth-century Germany (especially among Pietists), and, a century earlier, England gave us the first Quakers and the Anglican Nicolas Ferrar's beautiful experiment at Little Gidding. . . . It's hard to know when to stop adding to such a list, since such efforts are about as old as Christianity itself. But none of these communities is properly called monastic. Set the bar for monasticism as low as Wilson-Hartgrove sets it and you might as well call a Christian college dormitory a monastic institution. Frugality, fidelity, and consistency are very good things, maybe even essential things, but they aren't the same things as poverty, chastity, and obedience.

This is the point where I think we have to stop and ask what the heck is going on here. We have three books by very now-minded American Protestants who are noticeably eager to connect their projects to things ancient and, well, Catholic — or, at the least, pre-Reformational. And these books are by no means unique: it's worth noting that the same man who was so instrumental in calling evangelicals to a renewal of their worship lives, my late friend and colleague Bob Webber, spent the last years of his life promoting very similar ideas, which he gathered under the rubric of "the Ancient-Future Faith."

The connection to the ancient in all this is tenuous at best, but the earnestness with which it is proposed remains consistent. It's hard to say what's more curious, the earnestness or the tenuousness. Clearly these books and the general movement they represent constitute an attempt to borrow or transfer charisma: Ancient and monastic traditions of piety embody a community-building power and a devotional richness that these folks want to appropriate — but not at the cost of embracing either the doctrine or the authority of the Catholic Church or any other church. (Both McLaren and Wilson-Hartgrove invoke the example of St. Francis, but you'd never guess from either of them how anxious Francis was to get papal approval for his new community — how determined he was to be a faithful and obedient son of the Church.) A key assumption of all these books is that the beliefs and practices of other traditions that we like are detachable and transferable: It's a buffet, not a home-cooked meal. *Bricoleurs* love buffets.

New Monasticism strikes me as the most serious of these books because it confronts the possibility that you can't embrace certain practices unless your daily life takes certain specific material forms. Wilson-Hartgrove is careful not to allow anyone to think that he's telling them what they should or shouldn't do — all of these authors are utterly terrified of being judgmental about anything except (in Wilson-Hartgrove's case) the Bush administration — but, if living in modest and faithful community is just one option among many, the example loses a lot of its force. Whatever happened to comforting the oppressed and oppressing the comfortable? Wilson-Hartgrove should be as bold as Paul Farmer, the great doctor and advocate for the world's poorest, who says this about white liberals, whom he calls WLs: "I love WLs, love 'em to death. They're on our side. . . . But WLs think all the world's problems can be fixed without any cost to themselves. We don't believe that. There's a lot to be said for sacrifice, remorse, even pity. It's what separates us from roaches."

I suppose what I'm saying to all these authors is that I wish they would treat their own messages with more reverence and excitement — to see the "ancient church" as the radical challenge that it truly is. Think again of Paul Farmer. He doesn't say, "Here are some ways of helping the poor you might find helpful." He doesn't say, "I've chosen to live in a certain way, but I certainly wouldn't presume to tell anyone else what to do." Instead he says, with the poet Rilke, "You must change your life."

Some of Paul Farmer's political and religious beliefs strike me as misguided — he thinks Cuba an admirable regime, and he's a big advocate of liberation theology — but for a quarter century he has lived and worked in Haiti among the most miserable people in the Western Hemisphere. He has been their advocate, their doctor, and their friend. So when he speaks, when he says "You must change your life," I have to listen. Surely he has earned that much from me, that much at the least.

I am not saying that Halter and Smay and McLaren and Wilson-Hartgrove all need to be Paul Farmers before I will listen to them. There are hardly any Farmers in the world; he is an outlandish force of nature, as was Mother Teresa before him. Moral and spiritual heroism cannot be expected. But if "the ancient church," whatever that is, knew things about the faithful Christian life that we have forgotten, then for God's sake — and our own — let's hear about it. Let's hear it commended and celebrated, and let woe be proclaimed unto those who neglect it.

Must we change our lives? I fear we must. But how? There are, it seems to me, two general options. The first is that most radically Protestant of all models of sainthood, Kierkegaard's "Knight of Faith." There is nothing visible about this knight's sainthood; his transformation is purely internal. Kierkegaard's mouthpiece, Johannes de Silentio, scrutinizes the man: "I move a little closer to him, watch his slightest movement to see if it reveals a bit of heterogeneous optical telegraphy from the infinite, a glance, a facial expression, a gesture, a sadness, a smile that would betray the infinite in its heterogeneity with the finite. No! I examine his figure from top to toe to see if there may not be a crack through which the infinite would peek. No! He is solid all the way through." Will the knight of faith practice the spiritual disciplines? Certainly he will, but one would miss the point by naming them or treating them as tools or instruments toward the end of knighthood. The man's whole life is a discipline, the single one of devotion to his Lord. Purity of heart is to will one thing.

For some, the idea of imitating the knight of faith will seem too easy — after all, you can do it while living in a middle-class neighborhood in Copenhagen — but for the wiser it will seem too hard. Many monks and nuns say that they retreat to the monastic life because their faith is too weak to flourish in the *saeculum*. And if such a retreat, in any of its forms, is not as attractive to Christians as it once was, it may be because we have more protections than our ancestors did from an experience of utter exposure.

Some of our protections are material, some political, some psychological, but in any case the world has seen, over the past few centuries, a move from the "porous self" to the "buffered self." These are terms coined by the philosopher Charles Taylor. "The porous self is vulnerable," he writes, "to spirits, demons, cosmic forces" — and, I would add, to unpredictable natural forces and political authorities who know little or nothing of the rule of law. "And along with this go certain fears that can grip it in certain circumstances. The buffered self has been taken out of the world of this kind of fear."

The practices of the ancient Church were forged in eras of the porous self and were responsive to its fears and vulnerabilities. Can they be nearly as meaningful to us, surrounded by our protective buffers, as they were to our ancestors? Does their evident power suggest to us that we have paid too high a price for our buffers, that we may need to be more exposed? The self that can pursue the *via illuminativa* — that can be illuminated by God — may open itself to the demonic as well as the divine. The disciplines and practices of our Christian ancestors are not toys or tools; they are the hope of life to those who are perishing. This is what Alasdair MacIntyre had in mind when he said that, here among the ruins of our old civilization, what we may be waiting for is a new St. Benedict: someone who can articulate a whole way of life and call us to it.

The turn to the Christian past is indeed welcome, but it may demand more of us than we are prepared to give. In contemplating the witness and practices of our ancestors, we may discover that we'd rather remain within our buffers — if we can. But can we? Current electronic technologies — from blogs to texting to online banking to customer-specific Google ads — may be drawing us into a new age of porousness, with new exposures, new vulnerabilities. And in such a new age the hard-earned wisdom of our distant ancestors in the faith may be not just a set of interesting ideas and recommendations but an indispensable source of hope. Those who have ears to hear, let them hear.

Choose Life

In 2006 I was asked by Andy Crouch, on behalf of the Christian Vision Project, this question: How can followers of Christ be a counterculture for the common good?

IF WE eventually become a true counterculture for the common good, that counterculture (and that good) will simply be the product of our faithfulness.

Implicit in the question I have been asked to consider — "How can followers of Christ be a counterculture for the common good?" — is a judgment: that we followers of Christ are not now such a counterculture. It's a sound judgment, I think, and it seems to call for a particular kind of discourse: what that great scholar of early American culture, Perry Miller, called the jeremiad.

Miller tells us that the preachers of colonial New England, in an "unending monotonous wail," in "something of a ritual incantation . . . would take up some verse of Isaiah and Jeremiah with which to berate their congregants." After 1679 — thanks to the hard work of a synod of preachers — they could even employ a prefabricated list of the twelve varieties of iniquity characteristic of New Englanders, "merely bringing the list up to date by inserting the new and still more depraved practices an ingenious people kept on devising." Miller was duly impressed by these denunciations: "I suppose that in the whole literature of the world, including the satirists of imperial Rome, there is hardly such another uninhibited and unrelenting documentation of a people's descent into corruption."

Well, don't think I'm not tempted. But it would provide more pleasure for me than edification for my readers. The problem with jeremiads is that they only convince people already in the Jeremiah frame of mind; everybody else is likely to say, "Whoa, it's not *that* bad, is it?"

And in any case, those who would rectify the weaknesses or errors of any body of people should keep two warnings in mind. First, when a community fails to live up to its own standards, as of course it will, that community will be laboring under some kind of illusion — some distorted or fanciful self-understanding. As Kierkegaard pointed out long ago, "an illusion can never be destroyed directly, and only by indirect means can it be radically removed . . . one must approach from behind the person who is under an illusion." When anyone sees a jeremiad coming, he or she, like the captain of the *Enterprise,* immediately begins deploying the shields. This is why the prophet Nathan approached that adulterous murderer King David with a little story about sheep.

But the most desirable goods, like the most deadly illusions, rarely yield to direct assault. Wise men and gurus, saints and cranks alike testify that happiness cannot be sought but can only be found in the pursuit of something else. C. S. Lewis wasted years of his life seeking the peculiar stab of longing he called Joy — only to discover in the end that, like a stray cat, it declined to come when called, but appeared when it was least looked for.

Similarly, we Christians cannot set as our *goal* the becoming of a counterculture for the common good. Nor can we directly seek the elimination of the vices and illusions that constrain our attempts to love our neighbors as we should. We will strip away our self-deceit and become a true light unto the nations only by seeking and becoming *faithful* to the call of the Gospel. If we eventually become a true counterculture for the common good, that counterculture (and that good) will simply be the product of our faithfulness.

All too often Christians think even of faithfulness as a means to an end, that end being (usually) something called "church growth." We think so because in our culture goals are always *products:* quantifiable goods that, because they are quantifiable, can be produced by techniques. Thus our true ancestor is Charles Finney, the 19th-century evangelist who believed that his evangelistic techniques were fully scientific: "The connection between the right use of means for a revival and a revival is as philosophically [i.e., scientifically] sure as between the right use of means to raise grain and a crop of wheat." Improvements in agricultural technique and improvements in evangelistic technique are, then, achieved by application of the same experimental practices — though I am not sure what the evangelistic equivalent of Cyrus McCormick's reaper is. It is truly wonderful that Finney and his many modern heirs fail altogether to notice that whenever the Bible compares soul-winning to agriculture it invariably does so in order to emphasize the inscrutable sovereignty of God: Paul planted, Apollos watered, but God gave the increase. And we never get an explanation of *why* the ground on which the sower sows is so variable in quality, in receptiveness to the seed of the Gospel. Obedience, not results, must be our watchword, and in one sense all I have to say is this: be obedient to Christ today.

Last Christmas Day my pastor, Martin Johnson, spoke of his youthful habit of walking in the forests of British Columbia at night, guided only by moonlight. It was remarkable how far he could see by that meager illumination, how delicately beautiful the landscape was. The only problem was that he *couldn't* see where to put his foot for his next step, and as a result he took plenty of tumbles. The light of Christ, said Martin — the light that is Christ — is just the opposite: it illuminates with perfect clarity your next step, but blots out the surrounding territory. Christ is the Word of God, and the psalmist tells us that that word is a lamp unto our feet and a light unto our path: it shows us where to place one trembling foot, but it does not make us authoritative cartographers of the whole territory. It's worth remembering that when people ask Jesus the cartographic kinds of questions — "Will many be saved or only a few?" — Jesus tells them to mind their own spiritual business. I think that if we try to formulate a *plan* for becoming a counterculture for the common good — if we draw up a map and an itinerary — we may well receive a similar rebuke. "What is that to you? Follow me. One step at a time."

Yet there is a sense in which a focus on today's obedience makes a long view possible: it does not yield a map, but it does yield a confidence that he who has called us is faithful, and will conduct the whole Church to her journey's end. About a dozen years ago, Pope John Paul II agreed to answer some questions posed to him by an Italian journalist named Vittorio Messori. (His answers ultimately became the book *Crossing the Threshold of Hope.*) One of those questions concerned demographic predictions that Muslims would outnumber Catholics by the year 2000: "How do you feel when faced with this reality, after twenty centuries of evangelization?"

To this inquiry — with its freight of implicit worry — the pope replied placidly. After all, Jesus Christ himself proposed a still more frightening question: "When the Son of Man comes, will he find faith on earth?" (Luke 18:8) — will there be any faithful believers *at all?* And yet this same Jesus, John Paul reminded Messori, had already given this word of comfort to his fretful disciples: *"Do not be afraid any longer,* little flock, for the Father is pleased to give you the kingdom" (Luke 12:32, italics by JPII). The whole business of *counting* the adherents of religions in order to find out which of them "has a future" is a process at best distracting from, at worst hostile to, true faith.

The same trust prompts John Paul's successor Benedict to accept the possibility that the Roman Church may become smaller before it becomes larger. That is, the Church must insist on the integrity of its witness, because only such countercultural integrity will save the church — and therefore serve the common good — in the long term. Benedict has no interest in deliberately making the church smaller; rather, he wishes to make the church faithful, and if that has the (temporary) effect of reducing numbers, because there are people who will not wish to add to their lives the extra effort of becoming disciples, then so be it. One prays that this will not happen; one recognizes that it very well might. George Weigel points out that Pope Benedict is fond of quoting the old Benedictine maxim *Succisa virescit* — "pruned, it grows" — but as every gardener knows, the *immediate* result of a vigorous pruning is an apparently lifeless remnant: it is only in the next season that the luxurious growth appears.

Bodies of believers with a briefer history and shallower roots in the great tradition of Christian orthodoxy may find such assurance harder to come by. If we evangelicals habitually think locally and in the short term, that is because our very existence is local and short-term: we have to *will* a connection with historic orthodoxy. Still more must we pray for and earnestly seek the confidence that the Father is pleased to give us the Kingdom. And it is my belief that — both for our own well-being and for the common good — we need to find ways to *perform* the assurance that we are supposed to have, the confidence that the One who has called us is faithful beyond our ability even to imagine. Only when we act upon that assurance can we *enact a sign:* that is, only in that way does our confidence become readable. And what might such a sign be?

I think it would be wonderful if some large and wealthy American church would have to cut staff and programs (or better yet, actually have to close its doors) because it had given far too much money to foreign missions or the needs of local people. Not every such church, just one — or three or four, maybe — on the same principle that made my son's doctor, when Wes was five or six, check for the reassuring presence of cuts, scrapes, and bruises on his arms and legs: if he didn't have those, he was too timid. Unmarked limbs would have shown that Wes was keeping himself safe, but at the cost of failing to learn, failing to develop — failing, indeed, to find out what he *could* do as well as what he couldn't. How delightful it would be to drive past an empty megachurch and tell an unbelieving friend that the congregation couldn't pay their bills after they gave too much to rebuilding churches in New Orleans.

Or: given all the thousands of American churches that have enjoyed the great satisfaction of moving from a high-school cafeteria or a storefront to a beautiful new building, wouldn't it be wonderful if just a few reversed that course? That is, if a congregation gave their building away so that it could house a Christian service agency (or indeed another, poorer church), and then found a nice gymnasium somewhere to meet on Sunday mornings?

Some will say that such actions would be reckless and improvident, a failure to meet the standards of "good stewardship." But this would be to confuse the prudence appropriate to the monetary affairs of the bourgeoisie with the very different prudence called for by the Gospel. Compelling here are some words written by the Christian historian Christopher Dawson seventy years ago:

The spirit of the Gospel is eminently that of the "open" type which gives, asking nothing in return, and spends itself for others. It is essentially hostile to the spirit of calculation, the spirit of worldly prudence and above all to the spirit of religious self-seeking and self-satisfaction. For what is the Pharisee but a spiritual bourgeois, a typically "closed" nature, a man who applies the principle of calculation and gain not to economics but to religion itself, a hoarder of merits, who reckons his accounts with heaven as though God was his banker? It is against this "closed," self-sufficient moralist ethic that the fiercest denunciations of the Gospels are directed. Even the sinner who possesses a seed of generosity, a faculty of self-surrender, and an openness of spirit is nearer to the kingdom of heaven than the "righteous" Pharisee; for the soul that is closed to love is closed to grace.

Christians, I think, need to consider these words carefully. We must ask ourselves whether we have, indeed, taken "worldly prudence" for good stewardship, and Christian generosity for recklessness. And we must remind ourselves that we can insulate ourselves from surprising uncertainties or setbacks only by the kind of false prudence that insulates us also from surprising blessings.

Indeed, we need to ask what, exactly, in our prudence, we are afraid of. Sometimes I suspect that it is God himself, or at least life itself. Many years ago the farmer and writer Wendell Berry came across an advertisement for a new John Deere tractor heralding the advent of an "earth space capsule" that would protect the farmer not only from the "noise and fumes" produced by the tractor's own engine but also from the vagaries of weather. Berry found himself first bemused and then disturbed by the idea of a farmer who doesn't like weather; but then he reflected that this ad might well have relevance beyond the world of agriculture:

Of course, the only real way to get this sort of freedom and safety — to escape the hassles of earthly life — is to die. And what I think we see in these advertisements is an appeal to a desire to be dead that is evidently felt by many people. These ads are addressed to the perfect consumers: the self-consumers, who have found nothing of interest here on earth, nothing to do, and are impatient to be shed of earthly concerns.

Too many church buildings, it seems to me — and I say this suspecting that, for all my caveats and self-warnings, the spirit of Jeremiah has possessed me after all — have become vast "earth space capsules," and it may be time to escape before the spiritual oxygen runs out.

The sign I ask that some of us enact is not, I think, a sign of renunciation — not that there's anything wrong with that — but of generosity. Giving is not renouncing. And if it turns out that we cannot do this, or something like it, then I think the least we *can* do is to admit that we have locked ourselves in our capsules and have no intention of coming out. We can write our confession and tape it to the door so passersby can learn who we are.

Our great exemplar, I think, should be Yul Brynner. The Russian-born actor knew that he was dying from lung cancer when he appeared on ABC's *Good Morning, America* in January 1985. And on that occasion he said that what he really wished he could do was to tape a public service announcement that would say, "Now that I'm gone, I tell you: Don't smoke, whatever you do, just don't smoke." He died ten months later, and soon thereafter his words were indeed presented to the world by the American Cancer Society — prefaced by an image of his tombstone. So we too, we who could not manage to give or renounce, we who could not risk falling down, just before we crawl into our capsules should affix a simple message for those passersby, and especially for our children: "Don't do what we did. Don't hoard, don't close yourself up in your own comforts and even your own virtues. Be open to love and grace: choose life."